NEGOTIATE ! MANAGE ! SURVIVE !

HOSTAGE SITUATIONS

From Crisis Intervention to Dealing with Terrorists

Cecil Pearson and Eric Radli

LawTech Publishing Co., Ltd.

HOSTAGE SITUATIONS

Copyright ©1999 by Cecil Pearson and Eric Radli

QWIK-CODE is a trademark of
LawTech Publishing Co., Ltd.

Published by:
LawTech Publishing Co., Ltd.
1060 Calle Cordillera, Ste. 105
San Clemente, CA 92673

Phone: (949) 498-4815
Fax: (949) 498-4858
e-mail: lawtech@fea.net
Web site: www.lawtech.cc

10 9 8 7 6 5 4 3 2

p. 144

ISBN: 0-915905-98-1

ACKNOWLEDGMENTS

The authors wish to thank the numerous individuals who have supported us in many ways, from those who have supplied information during classroom settings, to the many colleagues we have worked with throughout the years. We have learned a lot. Special thanks to the following released hostages who shared their experiences with us: Dr. Karen Getney (Nevada State Prison), Susan Lundstrom (Nevada State Prison), Warren Maxim (Nevada State Prison), Doug Moore (Henry's Bar, Berkeley, Ca.). The information received from them was very helpful and beneficial in regards to the hostage survival material presented in this book.

A special thanks to Dr. Steve Graybar, Ph.D., for his contribution in the area of mentally disturbed inmates, and how law enforcement personnel should respond to them.

Lastly, thanks to Lt. Colonel J. B. Hopkins, USMC (Ret.) for his contribution in the area of hostage post-trauma care.

To Midge and Elsa,

For their support, optimism and patience...

But mostly for their love.

ABOUT THE AUTHORS

Cecil Pearson, Captain (Ret.), is a nationally recognized consultant and training provider in the areas of crisis and disorder management. He has extensive training in hostage negotiation. He is the founder and president of Cecil Pearson and Associates Inc.; a Las Vegas, Nevada based consulting firm. He has taught a variety of crisis topics to law enforcement agencies and private businesses for over 20 years. Pearson brings all of his training and experience to this book. Pearson is a graduate of the National FBI Academy and a member of the Police Writers Club.

Eric Radli, an active duty Lieutenant, has been involved in the field of hostage negotiations for over 17 years. Majoring in psychology, he has taught numerous seminars on hostage management, riot control, jail response teams, and first responder to the scene. Radli is a graduate of the FBI Hostage Negotiation Course. He has personally negotiated a large number of hostage-related incidents and has served as commander of a county Hostage Negotiation Team. His writing and teaching methods are direct, realistic and survival oriented. Radli is a two time inductee of Who's Who in American Law Enforcement and a member of the American Society of Law Enforcement Trainers (ASLET).

TABLE OF CONTENTS

CHAPTER 2: FIRST OFFICER ON THE SCENE

CHAPTER 3: COMMAND POST GUIDELINES

CHAPTER 4: INCIDENT COMMAND SYSTEM

CHAPTER 5: MEDIA RELATIONS

CHAPTER 11: THE DISTURBED HOSTAGE TAKER & THE NEGOTIATOR

CHAPTER 12: INTERACTING WITH EXTREMISTS/TERRORISTS

CHAPTER 13: LAW ENFORCEMENT & THE TERRORIST HOSTAGE TAKER

CHAPTER 14: HOSTAGE SURVIVAL - JAIL OR PRISON EMPLOYEES

CHAPTER 15: RELEASED HOSTAGES

CHAPTER 16: DEBRIEFINGS

INTRODUCTION

Hostage taking is on the increase across this country as well as around the world. This is of critical concern for law enforcement officers. Situations often occur which require either the use or threatened use of force and negotiation techniques.

Situations requiring the use of force or negotiation techniques may not always provide law enforcement personnel with adequate time to fully consider the benefits and drawbacks of all possible options. Policies and procedures should be developed to assist law enforcement officials in identifying circumstances, which may require crisis intervention, and to formulate strategies and options in advance of the hostage situation.

This book was written to provide the reader the knowledge of how to handle a hostage situation. It is intended to be a practical usable book designed to increase the understanding of how to respond, manage, and survive these types of incidents. Depending on the size and resources of the department, a patrol officer can potentially be a hostage negotiator.

Dating back to the beginning of recorded history, hostages have been taken for a variety of reasons with one unifying concept, which is, that a person is held prisoner until certain specified conditions are met. Since the early 1970's, hostage negotiations have taken the forefront as the preferred way to handle these types of situations. Not the only way, but indeed, the preferred way. During our forty years of involvement in this field in the law enforcement sector, we have been exposed to a wide variety of training and input from a number of sources. Very few of these were in written format. That is to say, we have attended numerous classes on this subject matter, but have noted very few texts covering the essential aspects of this volatile issue.

During our long involvement, we have instructed well over three hundred separate classes in all aspects of this topic. We have yet to discover a viable textbook to utilize in this effort. Additionally, there are none that we are aware of that actually contain an all-encompassing view of the subject.

Almost all classes we have instructed throughout the years have requested direction in obtaining a definitive textbook covering all the issues they were exposed to. We could only advise the students that such a book does not exist, but perhaps in the future, someone will author a book that covers all these issues. It now has come to a point for us to do something about this. Quite simply, to write a textbook.

The primary target group for this textbook is the actual practitioner. In other words, this book is aimed at those individuals who are involved in the successful outcome of hostage/hostage-related incidents. Mainly, these individuals will be found in the law enforcement community worldwide. Each agency large and small, has the real potential of being confronted with a hostage/hostage-related incident in today's society. One needs only to scan the newspapers to get a revealing indication of the propensity of something like this occurring in their workplace or neighborhood.

Almost on a daily basis, these types of incidents erupt causing law enforcement to respond the best way that they can. Indeed, there exist highly trained individuals, who are able to interact with the involved subjects based upon past training. Even through this may be the case, training comes at best far too infrequently, and continual updated training rarely occurs. When this is the case, written material in the form of a textbook is invaluable.

A secondary target group, albeit quite a large one, is the individual in the high risk jobs i.e.; bank employees, high profile business professionals, certain local, state and federal government employees, security personnel, etc. In short, the job position itself may project a possibility of being involved in a hostage incident. For example, a few years ago we instructed thirty-five Internal Revenue Agents in Hostage Survival and to our amazement found four of them to have actually been taken hostage during their career. We have noted the same situations with other training groups consisting of the aforementioned professionals.

This textbook is the definitive answer to many of the frequently asked questions during crisis training classes. Practitioners as well as potential victims will have the opportunity to reference material as they wish in order to maintain their proficiency or lower their risk of being victimized. In each case, individuals will be better able to handle hostage/hostage-related incidents.

The specific field of hostage negotiation was started in the early to mid 1970's by two individuals named, Dr. Harvey Schlossberg, Ph.D., New York Police Department (Retired), and Captain Frank Bolzs, New York Police Department (Retired).

Since that time, each of these individuals has written numerous articles and in Bolzs' cases, a book (Hostage Cop), covering various aspects of the subject. Each, have lectured across the country on basic hostage negotiation issues. This textbook is different from all other publications in that it covers information relating to the "entire" field of crisis incidents. We believe it offers insight, direction and procedure in areas of potential hostage/hostage-related incidents. From basic crisis intervention techniques to hostage survival and post trauma, this textbook is all encompassing in nature. In short, this book can be used as a complete guide in the field of crisis management and hostage negotiation and survival.

For continuity, suspects, hostage takers, etc., will be, for the most part, referred to in the singular even though there may be multiple individuals.

CRISIS INTERVENTION

In order to prepare oneself to confront and handle situations involving individuals involved in a crisis incident, a basic understanding of the principles of crisis intervention is necessary. Each day, everyone goes through some type of a crisis or problem, which may be classified as major or minor in nature. Most times, these are handled by relying on past experiences, training, inner resources or seeking the help of friends or professionals. When emotions overwhelm the ability to think and reason rationally, a crisis state occurs. When this happens, outside intervention in the form of clergy, doctors, friends, and sometimes law enforcement is often necessary.

Those working in emergency services or other high-risk positions may confront crisis situations on a daily basis because of the vocation in which they are employed. They may routinely encounter major life events such as births, deaths, major illnesses, fires, floods, robberies, hostage takings, etc. We must understand that a large number of crisis situations are caused by sudden unpredictable events, which call for immediate intervention. Because of all this, we must be aware of and skilled in the necessary procedures involved in handling individuals in crisis situations. Specifically, we must be able to identify, relate to and assist a subject who is going through a crisis.

CRISIS THEORY

At the beginning, we must start with the basic concept of crisis intervention, which is looking at an individual in a "Holistic" manner. That is to say, that one's personality should be seen as evolving through that person's life experiences. Along with this, the individual also develops what is known as a "Psychic System" which is the basis upon how he sees the world and in turn, determines how he acts. Biological, psychological and sociological experiences or events influence the psychic system. In short this is the total accumulation of life's experiences; a set of learned patterns of behavior.

With this in mind, we must remember that each and every individual has different psychic systems, based upon what they have experienced in their lives. Additionally, we must also acknowledge that we may come across people who have lived their entire life viewing certain things in a certain way. If that view does not conform to our own, we may encounter a problematic situation which may cause us to somewhat adjust our way of interacting. No matter how different their views may be, there are certain human needs, which remain consistent throughout the world.

HUMAN NEEDS

The primary basic human need is that of survival. If one's life is endangered, all other needs pale in comparison. However, if an individual's life is not threatened or in question, other types of needs may be viewed just as important as the need to survive. Psychological needs may assume a value as high as the need to survive. For example, these types of needs may take the form of the strong belief that one must eat three meals per day in order to survive. We all know that one will not die if they do not eat three meals.

The final type, of need which may assume a value as high as the need to survive are psychosocial needs. These needs may be defined as job security, love, peer group acceptance, respect, self-recognition and the desire to achieve. The key to understanding these needs is to keep in mind that everyone has different ones and may indeed place different levels of importance upon them. What may not be important to us may be extremely important to someone else.

NEED SATISFACTION SEQUENCE

Along with human needs embedded within each individual, there is also a definite "Need-Satisfaction Sequence" that everyone travels through each and every minute of each and every waking day. In other words, we all go through a specific process in order to attain necessary needs.

This process starts with a "Need" which is nothing more that some type of stimulus and tension. The amount of importance a person places on a particular need, will directly affect the amount of tension the person experiences; the more important the need, the higher the tension. This is followed by the "Action" part of the process. This is the thinking and evaluating portion of the sequence. Here, the individual thinks of the acceptable or in some cases, unacceptable behavior, which will satisfy the need. Next, the sequence moves to the "Process" stage. This is where the person actually takes the physical action to satisfy the need. The last part of the sequence is the "Satisfaction" stage. Simply, when the tension is reduced, the person experiences pleasure.

A simple example of the entire "Need-Satisfaction Sequence" may be found in an alarm clock awakening an individual. As the alarm sounds, the "Need" is to shut the alarm off. The "Action" is the thinking process which takes place in determining how to shut the alarm off.

The "Process" is the actual shutting off of the alarm. Finally, "Satisfaction" is reached when the alarm is off. As long as needs, are satisfied a person is able to function adequately. When needs are not satisfied or when they are satisfied by unacceptable measures, a crisis situation occurs. In short, our society places limits on how needs are satisfied. When these limits are passed, problems arise and a crisis develops.

IDENTIFYING CHARACTERISTICS

There are certain identifying characteristics associated with an individual who is experiencing a crisis situation.

Precipitating Event

The first characteristic is the presence of a "Precipitating Event," that one event which sends the individual over the edge into a full-blown crisis. This could be a divorce, job loss, or the death of a loved one. The specific event causes the individual to lose control of their emotional state. It is extremely important to note that the precipitating event does not actually have to be "REAL" in nature, just as long as the individual involved actually thinks it is real.

For example, an elderly person may call the police to report "Radar Men" being in their living room walls. The precipitating event is the "Radar Men." Upon arrival, the police officer listens to the story and advises the individual that he has something that will rid their house of the problem.

He then produces a large flashlight, turns it on and proceeds to walk around the living room with the light held against the wall. When finished, he turns the light off, returns it to his belt and tells the individual that the "Radar Men" are gone. The person expresses their thanks and the crisis is over; at least for now. Short-term solutions by officers in the field should be followed-up by referrals to the local Psychological Evaluation Team (PET), or other appropriate mental health agency for evaluation.

In short, the event was only real in the individual's mind, however the officer related to the crisis as though it were real. What is important is that the event was real to the individual involved.

Impaired Social Functioning

A second characteristic of a person going through a crisis situation is some type of "Impaired Social Functioning." This is a personality disorder similar to a phobia.

Non-Rational Emotional response

The third characteristic is some type of "Non-rational, Emotional Response." This occurs in a crisis state when emotions block the ability to think and act rationally. For example, if a person involved in a traffic accident gets out of their car and begins to kick the side of the car, that is an emotional response, but it may not be considered "Non-rational." On the other hand, if the person gets out of their car and begins to shoot the car with a handgun, that is "Non-rational" and in fact, can be classified as a crisis situation.

THE CRISIS

A "Crisis" is a functionally debilitating mental state brought on by a reaction to some event that a person believes to be so dangerous that it leaves them unable to cope by usual methods. A crisis is usually temporary in nature; it comes and goes in a short period of time.

If however, the crisis is allowed to continue without resolution, it can develop into a mental illness or some type of clinical disorder. As referred to in the previous paragraph, a "Functionally Debilitating Mental State" occurs when an emotional response overwhelms a person's thinking capacity.

One's emotions take control, up to the point of not actually being able to "Remember" how to take care of a crisis situation. For example, you may be a trained first aid provider but, when faced with your own badly injured young child, you become so overwhelmed with emotions you simply forget how to handle the situation. In most every crisis situation, there exists some type of "Anxiety." This is the innate physiological response to danger.

The Fight or Flight Response

Anxiety heightens the activity level of certain body systems and may appear as restlessness, agitation or hostility. The biggest problem we may face when interacting with individuals experiencing anxiety is that they may not even know what is causing them to feel anxious. How can we help if the person involved does not know what the basic problem is? We can start by knowing the methods used by people in dealing with their own crisis.

COPING MECHANISMS

There are many coping mechanisms which people employ in order to handle crisis situations they find themselves facing. Following is a short list of some of these:

Repression

This happens when unacceptable or unmanageable things are pushed into the unconscious part of the mind. In other words, the person experiences a failure to recollect certain past events.

Denial

Is when a person refuses to consciously admit that there is truly a problem. The feeling here is that if you do not admit there is a problem, you do not have to deal with it.

Displacement

This occurs when strong feelings are shifted from the original source or object to someone or something else. Many times this shift is placed on someone who has little ability to fight back.

Projection

This occurs when painful or unacceptable feelings are attributed to someone else, or simply blamed on someone else.

Regression

Is a person mentally returning to an earlier, immature mode of feeling and behavior. Here, an adult may actually think and behave as a juvenile.

All the above coping mechanisms are ineffective in that they are used as a substitute for realistic problem solving. They falsify reality and prevent the individual from assuming responsibility for their own personal behavior. Most all of these coping mechanisms fail to prevent the person from becoming overwhelmed by emotions. As stated previously, a crisis situation occurs when one's emotions overwhelm their ability to think and act rationally.

THREE BASIC CONCEPTS

When you come into contact with individuals who are experiencing some sort of crisis situations, you may be forced to interact with them in some way to try to assist them in regaining control. As a rule, there are three main areas to be concerned with in this type of situation.

First

You must strive to gain control of the incident that is to control the individual(s) involved as well as bystanders. Come across in a calm, concerned and reassuring manner.

Second

Attempt to guide the person into regaining control of their emotions and behavior. Try to identify the precipitating event and its meaning to the individual. Help the person see the "true" meaning of the event and how it actually relates to them. In short, help lead the person to a point where they can deal with the perceived threat leading to the crisis.

Third

If you are in a position to take appropriate law enforcement action, you should do so. If a crime was committed, enforcement action must be taken. Obviously, this is done after all those involved are least threatened.

WHAT TO DO

Crisis intervention incorporates a number of concepts regarding the effective ways of dealing with individuals. The following is a list of things to do when relating to a person in crisis:

Understand

Try to show an understanding of what the individual is experiencing. If the situation is unfamiliar to you, ask open-ended questions in an attempt to understand what is truly happening.

Empathize

Try to relate how you would react in this same situation, remembering that you are rational and the person involved in the crisis may not be.

Show Concern

Tell the individual that you truly care about their welfare. This may actually be very hard to do, especially if you are dealing with someone who has just injured or killed an individual. At times, you may have to play the role of an actor in order to promote the successful outcome of a situation.

Build Trust

Generally speaking, when you have built trust between you and the individual, you have effectively won. This is not to say that you will immediately end the incident but, at some point soon, if the individual trusts you, you will be successful. Trust is built by not being caught in a lie, keeping promises and continually interjecting during the conversation the phrase, "Trust Me."

Show Compassion

Reassure the person that they are okay and have value as a person. This may involve some "acting" on your part. Talk, get the person involved in a real conversation. Nothing can be accomplished until verbal interaction takes place. This may start with a discussion concerning something completely off the basic subject, however eventually the conversation will move toward the real issues at hand.

Listen

More important than talking is listening. Listen to what is being said as well as how it is being said. The same phrase spoken two different ways may have completely different meanings.

WHAT NOT TO DO

The following is a list of things not to do when relating to a person in crisis:

Over Stern

In general, at least at the start of the incident, try not to be over stern. Try not to give direct, one way orders, as this may upset the individual further and move them to some show of violence.

Indifference

When interacting with the individual, do not show an "I don't care" attitude. Come across as a caring person.

Indecisiveness

Show the individual that you are able to help them. Impress the person with your knowledge and show them that you know what you are talking about and that you have the answers and are indeed able to assist.

Carelessness

The most important concept to keep in mind when confronted with an individual who is going through a crisis is never, never become careless. Remember that all crisis situations have a potential for violence. Do not become over-confident.

This chapter was not written to make you a clinical psychologist, however it is extremely important to understand the basic philosophy behind how people think, act and react in certain situations. We must be aware of the possibilities of confronting individuals going through all types of crisis situations in the workplace or home and with that in mind, we must be capable of handling these situations. In short, the bottom line in all of these types of incidents is to be able to go home at the end of your workday.

CHAPTER 1 REVIEW QUESTIONS

1. What is the most primary, basic human needed?

   • Survival

2. True or False - If a crisis situation continues for a prolonged period of time and is not resolved, it may lead to a clinical mental disorder.

   • True

3. True or False - The fight or flight response is a sign of anxiety.

   • True

4. True or False - When relating to a person in crisis, you should be somewhat stern in nature. This helps in gaining control of the situation.

   • True

5. True or False - The most important point to keep in mind when confronting someone in a crisis situation is that if at all possible, you should never place yourself in a dangerous position.

   • True

FIRST OFFICER ON THE SCENE

Hostage incidents are increasing nationwide due to a variety of reasons. Waco, Texas involved religious beliefs. Hostage situations in prisons located in Atlanta, Georgia; Santa Fe, New Mexico and Lucasville, Ohio revolved around inmate unrest. Street officers often encounter hostage situations that begin as domestic violence calls. Hostage takings in businesses, schools, and during simple vehicle stops performed by our nation's law enforcement personnel are occurring more and more often.

Remain calm... the suspect is agitated, nervous, and unpredictable.
Calm him and the situation down. Speak in a slow, unemotional tone of voice.
Attempt to put the hostage taker at ease.

More violent criminals are accepting the concept of taking hostages as a means to their end. As a result of sophisticated communications systems, better alarm systems and faster response times, law enforcement officers are finding themselves confronting hostage incidents in the early stages. With this in mind, it is imperative that the first officer on the scene initiate appropriate action to control and eventually terminate the crisis.

As the first officer on the scene, the basic concept to understand and remember is that time is on your side. The longer the incident goes, the calmer it becomes. Time decreases anxiety and stress, while giving tactical and negotiating units a chance to setup, plan, and initiate specific techniques.

The rule of thumb in this type of crisis incident, is that unless someone (you, a hostage or bystander) is threatened with serious harm or death is to avoid aggressive assault on the hostage taker. This principle should remain intact until all other options are explored or attempted. When you have confirmed that hostages are indeed being held, a series of procedures must be set in motion.

First and foremost is the safety of the officer. Under no circumstances, if at all possible, should you place yourself in danger. Always seek cover. From a position of safety, attempt to block any escape path, which the hostage taker may use.

YOUR EXACT LOCATION

You should immediately advise the dispatcher of the following:

- The exact specifics of the incident

- The exact location of the suspect(s) and hostage(s)

- Any advisement or warnings to responding emergency units

After this is accomplished, the first officer on the scene must realize that they should assume command of the incident until relieved by a superior officer. This entails:

- Establishing perimeters, inner and outer

- Establishing a temporary command post

- Directing responding units to specific locations

- Evacuate non-affected civilians from the area (if possible)

VOLUNTEERS

Frequently, at the onset of a crisis incident, civilian volunteers might come forward to try to negotiate with the suspect. These volunteers may state they are acquaintances or relatives of the individual. Do not allow them to make contact with the suspect(s) due to the fact that they may aggravate the situation or push the suspect into more aggressive behavior. If possible, assign an officer to politely remove these helpful individuals who may distract you from your primary tasks. In short, as the first officer on the scene, your main goal is to "Control" the entire incident as best as you can.

INITIAL COMMUNICATION

The actions you take at a crisis incident may indeed set the stage for a successful outcome or on the negative side, a tragic conclusion. If pushed into a conversation with the hostage taker, under no circumstances should you promise anything. If promises are made at this point in time, further negotiations may be hindered. Additionally, never agree to change places with the hostage. This serves no purpose and quite possibly may be exactly what the hostage taker is hoping for.

Demands by Suspect

Most importantly, note any demands made by the suspect. Upon the arrival of the negotiators, these demands become extremely important in regards to understanding the motives and intentions of the hostage taker. For obvious reasons, never supply a weapon.

Discipline

As in all incidents of this nature, firearm discipline is extremely important. As the first officer arriving on the scene, tension levels are high, causing the possibility of emotional outbursts from all those involved. From a negotiator's viewpoint, words can always be taken back, bullets cannot.

Intelligence Gathering

Extremely important information, both tactical and situational, may be gathered and passed from the first officer on scene to additional responding unit, particularly the exact location of the hostage taker and the hostage.

Additional intelligence may include, but not be limited to:

- Description of suspect and hostage
- Detailed drawing of incident location
- Weapons present or available to the suspect
- And any injuries to any of the involved parties

It is important to remember that intelligence gathering is an ongoing process that consistently must be updated throughout the duration of the incident. In addition, it is imperative to assure that all involved personnel remain updated with current intelligence.

Effective gathering of any and all types of pertinent information is vital to the successful completion of a hostage incident. The first officer on the scene of a hostage incident may utilize a simple checklist:

- Locate the hostage taker(s)
- Locate the victim(s)
- Evaluate the incident
- Communicate pertinent information
- Isolate and control the incident
- Evacuate civilian personnel
- Resource: Neighboring department with trained negotiator

Sometimes, due to certain circumstances beyond your control, you may find yourself thrust into the position of actually negotiating with the hostage taker. Possibly, the suspect will initiate dialogue immediately upon your arrival, or your agency may simply not have a trained negotiator to send to the scene. Either way, you may need to employ certain basic techniques in speaking with the individual.

Remain calm

The suspect will most likely be extremely agitated, nervous and unpredictable. It will be your job to calm him and the situation down. Speak in a slow, unemotional tone of voice. Attempt to put the hostage taker at ease.

Endeavor to build trust

In other words, get the suspect to trust you and what you are saying. If possible, do not lie to him, or if you find that you must lie, do not get caught. With this in mind, when and if you tell a lie, make a note of it for future reference. Generally speaking, the minute you build trust and rapport between you and the hostage taker, it is hopefully only a matter of time until the incident is successfully concluded.

Be willing to listen to whatever is on the suspect's mind

This way, you are allowing the suspect to vent his anxiety level and in turn, calming the situation. Additionally, valuable intelligence may be obtained by allowing the hostage taker free reign to say what he wants.

Do not argue with the suspect

Try not to judge or condemn him, remembering that building rapport is a key step in negotiating.

Indicate that you are not in a position to make decisions

The hostage taker may attempt to make you grant certain demands made by him. Simply advice them that you are not in a position of authority therefore are unable to grant any demands without first checking with your superiors. Reinforce the concept that you can, on the other hand, guarantee the fact that he will not be harmed or killed. During the duration of the incident, keep in mind that your goal is to keep communications open. *As long as the suspect is talking, it is most likely that violent acts are not being performed.*

When the first officer on the scene makes contact with a hostage taker, the officer is betting that from this moment on their words and demeanor can prevent further violence and can set the hostage(s) free. Exactly what happens will depend largely on the negotiator's personal creativity, talent for persuasion, alertness, and knowledge of applied psychology.

If you as the first responder become a negotiator, you must appear to be a helpful middle person when talking to the suspect - someone who passes on problems and demands and who relays responses from superior officers. If you properly project sincerity, the suspect will accept you in an uneasy truce as a necessary instrument for his own well being. To open communications, choose a non-threatening positive statement.

Example: "I am here to help you."

This will allow firsthand intelligence gathering. Show interest in the suspect, giving him an opportunity to talk about himself. This can defuse tension and possibly reveal ways you might reach him, or buy time and establish that the negotiations are going to be a give and take situation.

BUYING TIME

As the first responder, reassure the suspect that the police do not want to harm him. No strategy for first responders to a hostage incident can be guaranteed to be "Fail Safe." Still, certain basic universal negotiation principles tend to serve most first responders in most hostage situations. Generally speaking, hostage takers fall into four broad, often overlapping categories:

1. Cornered criminals

2. Mentally disturbed persons

3. Inmates in jail or prison

4. Terrorists

Upon arriving at a hostage situation, you are most likely to encounter either the trapped criminal or the mentally disturbed individual. A hostage taker is often motivated by temporary mental breakdown connected with the trauma of trying to cope with society, feelings of inadequacy, a craving for power, chronic and severe mental illness, or real or imagined abuses by "The System." Terrorist's hostage takings are among the most difficult to handle and are the least likely to be encountered by most officers. They are especially dangerous because they carefully plan a hostage taking. A part of their strategy is a readiness to die for their cause. They often have ample weapons and outside support, and may be well trained and fearful of betraying their group. With all types of hostage takers, helping to buy time is one of the best contributions a first responder can make.

Hostage takers are most likely to talk sense with you as they have a chance to calm down and reassess their own situation. Any type of crisis incident tests the various capabilities of all those who are involved. A hostage taking, whether it is at a local convenience store or the county jail, is one of the most critical situations an officer may confront. As the first officer on the scene, your actions may prove to be the difference between life and death of the participants. As in many situations teamwork is essential. You, therefore become a vital link in this team effort and as such, must remain alert and skilled in the necessary functions of the first officer on the scene.

TIPS

1. Do not use a show of force. (It generally provokes the situation.)

2 Try to make as many notes as possible.

- Any responding specialized units will need this information.

- If you find yourself in a situation in which you must communicate with the bad guy, use active listening techniques from a position of cover.

CHAPTER 2 REVIEW QUESTIONS

1. Above all else, what is the main concern of the first officer on scene of a hostage/hostage-related incident?

   - Officer Safety

2. Basic information that should be obtained and passed on to your supervisor immediately upon their arrival on scene is:

   - Exact location of the incident Specifics of the incident

   - Location of the suspect and hostage

   - Warning to responding units

3. True or False - One concern of the first officer on scene is take command of the incident until relieved. This includes four (4) areas, one of which is to establish perimeters.

   - True

4. True or False - Obtaining a detailed drawing of the incident location is just one item in gathering of intelligence for the first officer on scene.

   - True

5. True or False - One prime directive to be utilized if the first officer on scene is forced into negotiating with the suspect is simply to attempt to build trust.

   - True

COMMAND POST GUIDELINES

This chapter will cover issues which should be acknowledged and addressed by command personnel at the scene of a hostage-related incident. While acting in that position, you must deal with multiple aspects related to tactical and negotiation operations in addition to critical activities of support personnel. Keeping mindful of the fact that every action creates a reaction, you must understand that the employment of a certain tactic or concept will result in some type of response from the suspect. Since each critical incident is different and unique unto itself, in the final analysis, whatever you as the commanding officer decide to do, based upon the maximum amount of available input, will play the decisive role.

Command Post personnel discussing options for an effective and justifiable conclusion to a crisis situation.

As an Incident Commander, you must be aware that hostages are taken for a variety of reasons. From violent domestic situations to planned political terrorist activities, mentally unstable or psychopathic individuals may chose to express themselves in this unacceptable manner. Because each type of suspect operates from different perspectives, the law enforcement response must take the individual's motivations into account. With this in mind, you must be flexible enough to act and react throughout the entire spectrum of possible responses to a suspect's actions. Ultimately, the primary goal and basic objective for law enforcement is always the same; the safe release of hostages and the taking of the suspect into custody.

OPTIONS

Generally speaking, you have five options available to you as the commander of this type of critical incident.

1. Contain, isolate and negotiate.

This action proves to have a very high success rate and therefore, is used by most agencies. One item that should be stressed is to "isolate" the suspect so that they can only speak to the negotiator. Situations have been known to go very badly when the suspect was able to contact the media, relatives, friends or associates. Control of this aspect is therefore, essential.

2. Contain, isolate and demand surrender.

This can occur during a barricaded subject situation where the individual is holding no hostages and the agency chooses to just "wait him out."

3. Employment of chemical agents to resolve the situation.

This is done when verbal tactics are not working and a decision is made to force the individual out.

4. Sniper to neutralize the threat.

You must keep in mind that accurate intelligence must be obtained in order to confirm the correct target.

5.   Send in the tactical team (SWAT).

This poses the highest risk to your personnel and to the hostages. Generally, if hostages are not being injured and there is no immediate threat to anyone, negotiations is the safest and preferred option.

PRIORITIES

To an untrained or uninformed individual, the concept of placing priorities on the elements of a crisis/hostage situation may result in the following scale:

- The life of the hostage is **first** priority

- The life of a bystander is **second** priority

- The life of the law enforcement officer is **third** priority, and finally

- The life of the hostage taker is **fourth** priority

In reality however, the command outlook should be; the life of the hostage is **first** priority, the life of a bystander is **first** priority, the life of the law enforcement officer is **first** priority and finally, the life of the hostage taker is **first** priority.

GUIDELINES

The following is a list of guidelines, which may be utilized by an Incident Commander during the set-up, operation and general response to a crisis/hostage incident. This list is not meant to be all inclusive and in turn, should only be used as a basic guide which can be adjusted and modified as one sees fit.

i.   Respond to the crisis with all necessary personnel and equipment. The initial main concern should be to contain, isolate and control the entire incident. Set up perimeters, cut off all forms of communication with the suspect to the outside world by forcing them to talk directly to you, over a secured line. In short, control all aspects of the scene.

2.   Establish a primary and secondary Command Post location.

3. Immediately formulate a Chain of Command by designating an Incident Commander and if necessary, instituting a formal Incident Command System.

4. Surround the incident with tactical personnel armed with suitable weapons and equipment to control entry and exit points along the perimeters.

5. Contact all emergency medical and utility company support personnel, and request their assistance at the scene. Confirm that adjacent law enforcement agencies are aware of the situation in case of mutual aid assistance becoming necessary.

6. Interview and debrief all witnesses and first responding officers who may furnish vital information regarding the specifics of the crisis incident.

7. Contact professional practitioners to assist in different aspects of the situation. Individuals such as psychologists, clergymen, probation/parole officers, etc. may be invaluable.

8. Activate the Public Information Officer to handle the media inquiries and issue statements throughout the duration of the incident.

9. Contact individuals who may be knowledgeable in the physical aspects of the building where the event is taking place. They will be able to furnish specific details regarding the physical lay out of the incident location and in turn, provide necessary intelligence to tactical personnel. Establish direct communication with the hostage taker as soon as possible through the use of a secured telephone line or an emergency "throw-phone." The "throw-phone" is a basic, self-contained telephone unit that is capable of maintaining a closed and highly controlled telephonic communication between two different locations.

10. If possible, establish a method of looking directly into the exact location of the incident. This may be accomplished by infiltrating the location with a fiber optical camera, mirrors or telephoto scopes.

11. In addition to the above, attempt to institute a listening device into the incident location. This will supply excellent intelligence information to the Command Staff.

12. Insure that verbal communication with the suspect is maintained. In other words, plan a back-up system to be used in case the primary communication system fails.

13. Initially, set no demands except for the release of hostages in return for meeting a demand from the hostage taker.

14. Accept no deadlines from the hostage taker. This may seem extremely difficult for you to do however; it is vital that Command Staff realizes that deadlines may be worked through. Nevertheless, generally speaking if the hostage taker injures or kills a hostage, as a response to a deadline not met, a tactical solution will most likely be necessary. In this case, negotiations should continue just to assist the tactical team in the performance of their task.

15. Remember that most every thing is negotiable except, ammunition or weapons.

16. Establish the methods necessary to deliver items to the suspect in safest, most effective manner possible.

17. If food is provided to the suspect, do not use drugs to taint the edibles. Normally, the hostage taker will require the hostage to taste the items prior to his ingestion.

18. Avoid providing alcohol to the suspect.

19. Do not permit anyone to exchange themselves for the hostage being held. This may make the situation worse by providing a hostage more important to the hostage taker than the initial person held captive.

20. Request to view the hostages to determine their welfare. However, do not show over concern for them. By exhibiting over concern, you actually increase the importance of the hostage in the eyes of the suspect, thereby giving them a perception of increased power.

21. Be prepared to employ tactical measures immediately if the hostage taker begins to injure his hostage. This decision should be weighed against the possibility of the hostage taker continuing to harm the individual or others.

22. Continue to assess the situation evaluating the aggression potential of the suspect, i.e. can they actually do what they are threatening to do? Is the willingness to negotiate still evident? Is the suspect maintaining rationality?

23. The basic rule regarding this type of incident is if the suspect is talking with you, he is not harming someone. Therefore, keep the suspect talking. By doing so, the opportunity for a successful outcome remains open.

24. Do everything that is possible to consume time. Generally speaking, the longer an incident goes, the more likely it will end by successful negotiations. Time allows tension and stress to subside.

25. Some demands are actually "giveaways." In other words, a demand for food, cigarettes, a meeting with the media is easily met and in turn, builds rapport and trust. This will aid in the successful outcome of the incident.

26. If a decision is made to end the incident through tactical action, be decisive and determined to complete the action once it is started. Recognize that this move is a "showdown" and in turn, based upon the suspect's irrational and destructive actions.

Utilizing these guidelines will not automatically ensure a non-violent, successful outcome to an incident. These concepts will, however, form a strong basis to build a response that is effective and oriented toward a safe and justifiable conclusion to a crisis situation.

CHAPTER 3 REVIEW QUESTIONS

1. What type of action has been proven to have a very high success rate and is used by most agencies?

    *   Contain, isolate, and negotiate.

2   What is the primary goal and objective for law enforcement?

    *   The safe release of hostages and the taking of the suspect into custody.

3. True or False - Utilizing guidelines will not automatically ensure non-violent successful outcome to an incident. They will, however form a strong basis to build a response that is effective and oriented toward a safe and justifiable conclusion to a crisis situation.

    *   True

4. True or False - You must deal with multiple aspects related to tactical and negotiation operations in addition to critical activities of support personnel.

    *   True

5. True or False - Sending in the tactical team FIRST is the preferred option.

    *   False

INCIDENT COMMAND SYSTEM

During any type of critical incident, instituting and maintaining control is of the utmost importance. In 1970, Southern California was hit with a series of devastating fires. Hundreds of thousands of acres were burned, hundreds of structures were destroyed and numerous lives were either lost or forever changed. Because of this, the Incident Command System (ICS) was developed.

The U.S. Forest Service began to research management systems that would assist fire-fighting agencies in improving their coordination and effectiveness and in short, provide a better means of handling emergencies. Ultimately, the ICS was born and has proven to be the most efficient and effective critical incident management system. In 1974, the San Bernardino County Sheriff's Department reviewed and modified the existing ICS to make it more adaptable to law enforcement.

Incident Command System (ICS) personnel mapping out strategies, making decisions, and implementing plans.

Considering the varied needs of police agencies in regards to responding to both natural and man made emergency incidents, the Sheriff's Department studied numerous systems both within the state and across the nation. In its final analysis, completed in 1995, we find a relatively simple concept, based upon the original fire system program. The present law enforcement Incident Command System is able to be used and has been used in everything from a suicidal, barricaded person to a major earthquake.

BASIC COMMAND STRUCTURE

Incident Commander

The Incident Commander has complete authority and responsibility for the overall operation of the situation. All strategic decisions and implementation of plans and resources fall under their control. General responsibilities may include, but are not limited to:

- Setting up a Command Post

- Obtaining and assess the present status of the incident

- Assigning Command Staff and section Officers in Charge

- Conducting initial briefing

- Activating the ICS

- Approving and authorize an Action Plan, keeping in mind that a written plan is preferred, but not always necessary

- Determining needs and coordinate staff activities

- Delegating when appropriate

- Approving requests for additional resources and personnel

- Authorizing media releases

- Approving Action Plan and forward it to appropriate agencies

- Approving plans for demobilization

Deputy Incident Commander

The Deputy Incident Commander assists the Incident Commander and is authorized to direct the incident when taking over the duties of the Incident Commander during their absence. Depending on the type of emergency, the Deputy Commander may handle subsequent incidents originating from the initial emergency. For example, a major crime may occur during a fire.

The Incident Commander may manage the fire response after which the Deputy Incident Commander may handle the criminal response. In other words, the transition of authority and responsibility from one jurisdiction to another is made efficiently with little disruption of services.

Safety Officer

The duties and responsibilities of this position may include:

- Overseeing all safety procedures and practices

- Monitoring and assess safety hazards, which may develop during the incident

- Developing measures for ensuring personnel safety

- Correcting unsafe acts or conditions as necessary

- If necessary, the Safety Officer may exercise emergency authority to stop or prevent unsafe acts when immediate action is required

Operations Officer

The Operations Officer activates and supervises the operational elements of the Incident Action Plan. They coordinate tactics, resources and changes to the plan as they may arise, and report to the Incident Commander. Responsibilities include:

- Obtaining briefing from the Incident Commander

- Providing input to the Action Plan

- Keeping the Incident Commander advised of the organization and deployment of field forces

- Recommending general areas for staging of personnel and equipment

- Establishing perimeters and evacuation plans as necessary

- Furnishing the Incident Commander with unit designations and areas of responsibility

- Continually monitoring chain of command and span of control for efficiency

- Assuring effective communications

Staging Manager

The Staging Manager coordinates and stages resources. Their responsibilities and duties may include:

- Obtaining a briefing from the Operations Officer

- Establishing and supervise Resources Unit

- Establishing Staging Area layout

- Determining needs for equipment, food sanitation, and security

- Establishing check-in procedure and obtain equipment as needed

- Requesting maintenance for equipment if necessary

- Coordinating and establish tracking for issued equipment

- Tracking and reporting any resource change in status

- Maintaining a unit log

Planning/Intelligence Officer

The Planning/Intelligence Officer obtains and provides information regarding the current situation, attempts to predict future course of events, and provides strategy to control the event. Responsibilities and duties may include:

- Obtaining a briefing from Incident Commander, especially on the operational objectives

- Establishing reporting schedules for the unit officers to use in preparing the Incident Action Plan

- Supervising the preparation of the Action Plan

- Assembling information on alternative strategies

- Identifying the need and source of specialized resources

- Performing periodic predictions on the incident potential

- Compiling and display the incident status summary

- Advising units of incident status summary

- Provide an incident traffic plan

- Preparing and distribute the Action Plan

- Coordinating the release of unnecessary resources after approval by the Incident Commander

Check-in Recorder

The Check-in Recorders are assigned to each check-in area to ensure that all resources are accounted for. Responsibilities and duties may include:

- Obtaining a briefing from the Resources Unit Coordinator

- Establishing communications with the Dispatch Center

- Posting signs so arriving units and resources can easily find their designated areas

- Transmitting check-in information to the Resources Unit on a regular schedule

- Forwarding completed lists and status changes to the Resource unit

Public Information Officer

The Public Information Officer formulates and supplies pertinent information to the media. Responsibilities and duties may include:

- Obtaining a briefing from the Incident Commander

- Contacting and coordinate with the jurisdictional agency Public Information Activity

- Establishing a Incident Information Center ideally away from the Command Post

- Preparing an information summary as soon as possible

- Obtaining approval for information releases from the Incident Commander

- Attending meetings to update information as needed

- Releasing news to representatives from the media

- Arranging for meetings between the media and Incident personnel authorized by the Incident Commander

- Providing escort service for the media and VIP's

If an emergency situation continues for some time, the Incident Commander may wish to institute a Financial Officer. During certain situations, agencies may find that specific funds allocated to the solution of the incident may be recouped from the Federal Government, such as in the event of a devastating flood. No matter what the incident may be, the incident Command System is a valuable and necessary tool.

CHAPTER 4 REVIEW QUESTIONS

1. What law enforcement agency reviewed and modified the Incident Command System to what we use now?

   • San Bernardino County Sheriffs Department

2. True or False - During a crisis situation, the Incident Commander is in charge of all aspects of the Incident.

   • True

3. What section provides the point of contact for mutual aid units?

   • Liaison Officer Section

4. What section establishes check-in procedures and obtains equipment?

   • Staging Manager Section

5. True or False - Agencies may be able to recoup funds, which were spent during a major incident, such as a flood.

   • True

MEDIA RELATIONS

During and immediately after any type of crisis situation the news media is ever present. They are the watchful eye of the public, the reporters of the facts and the advisors of the immediate community. Communicating with these individuals can be a stressful and sometimes frustrating experience. We must accept the fact that we provide the information to the media who then report it. With that in mind, we must also remember that we are therefore expected to perform our role to the best of our ability.

For the most part, reporters are fair and are simply interested in obtaining a story for their network. They are concerned about all aspects of a situation and are eager to interview the persons who can supply the necessary information. Reporters are looking for the five or ten second interview with someone who is direct, clear and informative, and answers the important questions. They want to deal with someone who is also aware of the time constraints and deadlines placed upon reporters by their networks. Our responsibility is to provide and present the facts, background and our point of view regarding the crisis situation we find ourselves facing. With all of this in mind, a number of basic points should be noted and followed.

INTERVIEW PREPARATION

Prior to any interview, it's imperative that the spokesperson be prepared. The following checklist should be used as a way of getting ready for an interview:

- Be familiar and operate within your department's guidelines regarding media contacts

- Know your department's policies and procedures particularly regarding special unit operations and hostage situations

- Get your facts straight - get briefed by the Incident Commander

- Determine what information may be released to the press - do not compromise the incident

- Jot information down, particularly information regarding numbers - don't trust your memory

- Anticipate questions using "worst case scenario"

- Check your grooming and personal appearance

- Don't be pressured into conducting an interview until you are thoroughly prepared

- Employ self-calming techniques prior to interview

Release news to the media in a professional and timely manner.

OTHER IMPORTANT CONSIDERATIONS

Get Your Message Across

Be prepared to say what you want to say, understanding that you will have to answer the reporter's questions. You are the expert in this type of situation, so take the initiative and get your message across. If given the opportunity, prior to the interview, think about the key issues and statements you wish to present. This way, you can work those issues and statements into the interview when and where appropriate.

Be Informative

Media interviews are not meant to be "conversations" with the reporter. You are there to forward information to the public. Do not feel as though you must be entertaining or carry on a formal conversation. Do not be drawn into a long rambling message in response to a question; this may in fact dilute the impact of your original statement. Always be security minded, not revealing information that would be helpful to the suspect who may just be watching your interview on TV.

Be Brief

The media, especially television, is looking for a quick statement or series of statements to be used in a 5-20 second sound bite. Keeping this in mind, prepare and know what you want to say prior to the interview. If you use the seconds, which are allotted to you wisely, the more likely your message will get on the air.

Do Not Go "Off The Record"

There is actually no such thing as being "off the record" when speaking to the media. If you are confronted with this issue, understand that even if the reporter does not use your name as a direct source, they may use the information you supply to confirm or substantiate a story from another source. The best advice to be mindful of is that if you do not want to see your information reported, do not offer it.

You Are The Spokesperson

An interview is not the place to express your own ideas and opinions. The public will be interpreting what you say as a statement from your agency. If at some point you are asked a question that you do not know the official response to, do not speculate. Find out your agency's position and report it at a later time.

Information Continuity

Ideally, there should be only one spokesperson. This effectively eliminates the chance that conflicting information will be released to the media.

If more than one person is commenting on the incident, the public information officer should ensure that the statements issued do not conflict with or contradict one another.

Do Not Use Jargon

As in any profession, law enforcement uses its own special type of language with its acronyms and other numerical abbreviations, which may be and often are, unfamiliar to the general public. An interview containing this type of language is ineffective and reinforces negative police stereotypes. Do not use any type of wording which will require some type of explanation for understanding. Avoid police-type words such as, exited, proceeded, initiated or altercation. Words such as these are frequently found in the "words not to use list" in modern report writing texts.

Tell The Truth

In all situations, tell the truth. It may hurt, but it will never hurt as much as being caught in a lie. Always being truthful and honest will gain you and your agency credibility with the media, even if the answer is "No, I don't know the answer to that question, but I'll find out later" or "I can't answer that question at this time." If you can't answer a question, explain why. If there has been a negative event for your department, counter with a positive statement regarding what is being done about the problem. However, don't tell them that you are doing something that you are not really doing. The lie is often worse than what it is you're lying about.

Do Not Lose Your Temper

There may be times when a reporter attempts to provoke you into supplying a heated response to a question. This may be for dramatic effect of used at a later date asking you to explain your previous angry response. In either case, you come across as someone who cannot control situations.

Be Professional

An interview should be a friendly interaction between you and a reporter. This is accomplished simply by being professional, tactful and not confrontive. This builds rapport. Treat reporters fairly and equitably showing no favoritism. An interview is not an interrogation. Conduct the interview when "you' are ready. Don't be pressured by the press to give a statement when you are not fully prepared. Adjust your demeanor to fit the event.

Never Say "No Comment"

A response stating "no comment" may, and many times will, be interpreted by the public as being evasive and used to cover up something the agency does not wish the public to know. The best way to handle this is to state the specific reason why you cannot answer the particular question.

Be Confident

In these types of situations, keep in mind that you are the expert. In some cases, the reporter may be the individual who is somewhat intimidated and in fact, must be put at ease. Keep in mind that building a good rapport with the reporter can only help.

Be Aware Of When You Are Being Taped

Whenever the media is near, you can rest assured that either a tape recorder or video camera is in use. Always assume that you are on tape and act accordingly. Television camera crews will frequently film background shots, possibly with you and your personnel in view. Do not be captured on film acting unprofessionally.

It Is Okay To Make A Mistake

We are only human. During a taped interview you may feel as though you have gotten into a situation where you don't really know what your are saying, or in fact, you have stated something incorrectly. Just explain to the reporter that you did not really answer the question very well and you would like to re-tape it. Usually, the reporter will welcome a better and well thought out second take. However, if it's a live interview, make sure that you're well prepared.

CONTINUING AND FOLLOW-UP INFORMATION

Continuing Information

During a crisis incident, it is extremely important to include the media and in turn the public. You must keep the community informed as to the extent of the incident and its effect upon their lives. To do this effectively, a Press Station should be established in a location away from the Command Post area. This is where all the media should be directed for updates of the incident. Regular reports should be given at scheduled times throughout the duration of the crisis. This will keep the reporters at that location instead of having them move in and around the scene. It is imperative that reports are given to the media on a regular basis, thus keeping the community informed of the events while at the same time preventing the media from obtaining inaccurate information.

Prior to a crisis actually occurring, a Crisis Communication Plan should be created covering all of the above issues. Once a crisis happens, respond to the media as quickly as possible; the longer you delay, the harder they will strive to obtain information. This may be the worst case scenario in that the media will be unforgiving in their reports on your side of the story. Make their job easier if you can. Try to assist them in obtaining pictures and information. In this way, rapport is built and in the long run, your job is made easier.

If there are major meetings with the press, prepare for them. Review key points, which you wish to pass on. If possible, hold a dress rehearsal with your staff so that you may prepare responses to specific questions while at the same time, critique performance. Learn from your mistakes and act in a humane manner.

Follow-up Information

After the conclusion of the incident and all personnel have been debriefed and all the issues have been reviewed, the press should be given an "Incident Clarification Debriefing" outlining the actual facts of event.

Media Log

Lastly, maintain a log of each media interaction. This will be extremely valuable in evaluating the progress of the situation with regards to community involvement, while supplying up-to-date information for necessary personnel to review. Working with the media can be accomplished with a little effort and a great deal of preplanning.

Planning this prior to a crisis incident erupting will be nothing but beneficial to both the media and your agency. Remember that it's all about getting your point across in an effective and informative manner. To do so will contribute to a win-win situation.

(For a more in depth guide to working with the media, refer to *Media Survival for Law Enforcement Officers*, published by LawTech. See outside back cover for contact information.)

CHAPTER 5 REVIEW QUESTIONS

1. True or False - During an interview, there is really no time that you are "Off the Record."

    • True

2. The media is generally looking for a quick informational sound bite for broadcast purposes. This is usually how long in length?

    • 5-20 seconds

3. True or False - It is quite acceptable to use as much "Jargon" as possible during an interview. This shows the public how experienced you are in turn, someone they can trust.

    • False

4. True or False - The response, "No Comment", should never be used, it may be inferred by the public as being an attempt to cover-up something.

    • True

5. True or False - If there is a chance prior to a press conference, never formally practice your responses to stated questions. This may cause you to appear "Too Prepared" during the actual conference and in turn, come across as being "Too Stiff."

    • False

HOSTAGE - INCIDENT RESPONSE

Law enforcement and correctional officers are usually responsible for the initial response at the scene of hostage incidents. To clearly understand your role in such situations, you must be familiar with the tactics of hostage takers and the procedural steps involved in the negotiation process. Such knowledge may help to save the lives of hostages, bystanders, and fellow officers.

Since 1968, hostage taking by political extremists and criminals has steadily increased, and there is every indication that the frequency of hostage incidents will continue to rise. The most notorious incidents are international hostage takings for political purposes, a matter in which most law enforcement agencies will not likely become involved unless your agency is located near a sensitive government or political installation.

Nevertheless, you should be familiar with the tactics of the political extremist since their methods are being employed increasingly by criminals and others in situations where local law enforcement personnel are responsible for intervention. You should be prepared to respond to armed robbery attempts where bystanders have been seized to aid criminal flight, to jail and prison disorders where hostages have been taken, or to family disputes and highly emotional situations where violent individuals hold victims for irrational reasons.

THE PERPETRATORS

For you to effectively intervene in hostage taking incidents, you should be aware of the general characteristics of those who most frequently engage in such acts. Knowledge of the hostage taker's characteristics helps to determine whether the negotiation process is feasible or whether an immediate tactical response is required. Those who are most frequently involved in hostage taking are generally classified as terrorists, escaping felons, rioting inmates, and emotionally violent individuals. Within these broad categories are certain diagnostic characteristics that we will examine in Chapter 11.

Terrorist

The terrorist poses the greatest of threats because he is often fanatical to the point of murder and suicide. Terrorists may also use unknown accomplices outside of the hostage incident to influence public opinion and to exert pressure upon law enforcement to meet their demands.

When a terrorist group holds hostages and makes nonnegotiable demands for the release of prisoners, provision of weapons, or promise of amnesty, they should be advised at the outset that these demands will not be met. Once the terrorists become aware that these demands are nonnegotiable, an immediate impasse is reached and they are left with a limited number of options. The terrorists can choose to kill the hostages and commit suicide, which is unlikely, they can surrender, or they can lessen their demands to more realistic proportions and enter into negotiation.

Although some fanatical terrorists will not lessen their demands because of strong commitment, most terrorists will react to the reality of the situation and negotiate. Once terrorists admit that they are willing to settle for less than initially demanded, you have gained the psychological advantage and negotiation is possible.

Escaping Felon

Quicker response by law enforcement has increased the occurrence of confrontations between officers and felons at crime scenes. When felons feel trapped at a crime scene, they sometimes choose to seize hostages to use as shields during escape attempts or to barter for their freedom. The "Three Strikes and You're Out" sentencing guidelines instituted in some states may contribute to the desperation of criminals who don't want to be put away for life.

Since the felon's act of taking hostages at a crime scene is aimed toward a rational end, of safety and freedom, it can be assumed that negotiations are possible with this type of criminal. Initially, however, the situation poses a real threat to the safety of the hostages if the felon is caught in an unplanned situation is confused, frightened, and fearful for his own safety. He is being forced to make snap decisions in a crisis without the opportunity to assess the situation realistically.

At this point, you should suggest that he "cool off," analyze his position, and reflect on the consequences of his acts. This serves to channel the criminal's thought in the direction of negotiation. Once the situation has stabilized, preliminary negotiations can begin.

Armed felons who take hostages when trapped often imitate the behavior of political terrorist. Terrorist rhetoric is employed to make their position appear uncompromising. In such cases, the criminal's convictions should be doubted, if their original actions have no political overtones. The rhetoric is probably more of a bargaining tool than an expression of deeply held commitment.

Inmates

Our nation's jail and prison systems house the most violent and uncontrollable examples of our society. Oftentimes, these individuals attempt to gain control over their environment by taking hostages, destroying property and issuing demands. They may demand release, better food, better living conditions, changes in institutional policies or any other concern they deem essential. These inmates may truly feel they have nothing to lose and everything to gain therefore, in their minds their actions are justified.

In most hostage situations, time is on the side of law enforcement however, when dealing with inmates, this concept may not necessarily be the case. The longer an incident within a correctional facility is allowed to continue, the more organized the inmates may become. Additionally, an incident that is allowed to go on for an extended length of time within a penal institution may allow the disturbance to spread, involving more of the facility. This in turn, may create a harder situation for responders to handle. With this in mind, immediate intervention may be necessary and desirable.

Local law enforcement officers (patrol, SWAT teams, etc.) are called to intervene in jail and prison hostage situation when correctional personnel feel that additional manpower is needed to control disturbances. The Manatee County Sheriff's Office in Florida, has a very unique program whereby, the CERT team trains and practices with the Jail Response Team. The use of such a program is viewed by both law enforcement and correctional administrators as being highly desirable and effective.

Mentally Deranged

Increasingly common are incidents where a mentally ill person takes individuals as hostages. Extreme care in these situations must be exercised since the disturbed person is not capable of acting rationally. You should attempt to identify and reduce the emotional stress that is usually the precipitating factor in these incidents. The passage of time in itself usually helps to reduce the hostage taker's anxiety. You should maintain a calm attitude and avoid any acts that may threaten an emotionally ill person.

CHAPTER 6 REVIEW QUESTIONS

1. For you to effectively intervene in hostage taking incidents, what is one issue that you should be aware of ?

   • Basic hostage taker characteristics

2. Who is usually responsible for the initial response to the scene of hostage incidents?

   • Law enforcement and correction officers

3. True or False - It is not important for you to be familiar with the tactics of the hostage taker and the procedural steps involved in the negotiation process.

   • False

4. True or False - You should be prepared to respond to armed robbery attempts where bystanders have been seizes to aid criminal flight, to jail and prison disorders where hostages have been taken, or to family disputes and highly emotional situations where violent individuals hold victims for irrational reasons.

   • True

5. True or False - Terrorists may use unknown accomplices outside of the hostage incident to influence opinion and to exert pressure upon law enforcement to meet their demands.

   • True

HOSTAGE TEAM DEVELOPMENT

Effective Hostage Teams do not just happen by accident, but instead are created by diligent selection, planning and preparation. This concept must start from the top of the agency and extend down through all of the ranks. In other words, for a Hostage Team to be born, policies and procedures must be developed which outline the specifics surrounding all aspects of the process. Upper management must embrace the basic idea that there exists a need for a team of this nature to work in conjunction with a Tactical Team. Once this idea is accepted, the work actually begins.

SELECTION PROCESS

Volunteers

Without a doubt, the most important aspect of building a Hostage Team is that of selecting the right personnel to fill the roles. To begin with, as opposed to assigning individuals to this type of team, volunteers should be gathered. That is not to say that if there is an individual who shows some type of talent that would be beneficial for the team, they should not be recruited. In fact, these individuals can be great assets, depending upon their talents.

Gender

Both male and female personnel should fill membership slots on every Hostage Team. Depending upon the situation you are facing, one or the other sex may perform better, oftentimes dictated by the individual involved. For example, if a male subject runs his family out of his house at gun-point because of a problem with his wife, a female negotiator may not be effective. On the other hand, if a male subject is threatening suicide, he may feel closer to a female voice thus, creating a bond or trust quicker than a male negotiator might.

Race and Ethnicity

If possible, a variety of ethnic and racial groups should be reflected on these teams, especially if you are located in an area of the country that has a cross section of different races and ethnicities. It could be extremely difficult to communicate with individuals speaking a different language than yours. Further, numerous problems arise when you cannot relate to someone due to the fact of different cultural value systems being in play. If you are unable to recruit these type of members, attempt to locate a nearby language bank and form an alliance with them so that during a crisis situation you can make contact and utilize their expertise. Most colleges or universities have these banks and are more than eager to assist. Larger cities frequently have certified court translators who are often used by hostage teams as a resource.

Age

In an attempt to broaden the base of your team, members should represent a wide range in age. This will allow flexibility when dealing with a subject. If a young subject is involved, a young negotiator may be more effective than one who may be a reminder of a parent. Conversely, if the subject is a Vietnam veteran, someone of like experience may be better able to relate to the problem being faced thus, be better able to build a strong bond and trust.

Other Resources

To further the concept of broadening your team base, a representative of the psychological community, a psychiatrist or psychologist, would make an effective member. This individual can provide invaluable insight into the psyche of a subject in a crisis situation. Team members may draw upon the wealth of knowledge of these individuals and in turn, employ effective verbal tactics suggested to them. Additionally, someone who is knowledgeable in theology, such as a chaplain or priest, may be useful from time to time.

Skills

Obviously, team members must be good communicators and possess good common sense. Their ability to think on their feet, be resourceful, persuasive and able to function well under stressful situations are all vital attributes of good team members. With this in mind, recommendations from the applicant's supervisors are helpful in the selection process. Past performance is a sound indicator of future action. Ultimately, a psychological test may be administered to all applicants to confirm their suitability for the position.

TRAINING

You may have the best cross section of team members possible, however if they are not adequately trained, success is but an empty wish. As in many topics, training becomes one of the most important factors to be addressed. From the Administrative viewpoint, this factor covers major liability issues that will surface at the conclusion of any crisis incident involving your personnel. The question will always be, "What training has your team and individual personnel received?" Additionally, you will be expected to produce written documentation of any and all type of training provided to your personnel. If your training program falls short of what is considered "minimal," your liability will grow.

All of the concerns then come down to one basic question: "What training is essential for Hostage Team members?" Starting at the beginning, instruction in the principles of "Crisis Intervention" should be afforded to all members of the team. This will set the stage for all additional training classes. Everyone must begin with a basic understanding of the issues surrounding crisis situations and how different individuals react to them.

A course covering the "First Officer on the Scene" must also be supplied so members can review the necessary requirements of that position and how it relates to their team. This covers the beginning of the interactive process between the suspect and those attempting to help.

The basic techniques involved in the negotiation procedure should include suspect profiling, negotiating guidelines, use of specialized equipment, and specifics regarding the role of the negotiator. These concepts must be instilled in team members until they become second nature. All of this should constantly be reinforced through the use of operational scenarios and role playing exercises. Keeping in mind that practice makes perfect, training exercises should be scheduled as on-going events. In other words, Hostage Team members should train on a regular basis, ideally monthly, and above all they should train as a team.

Another issue is that whenever possible, the Hostage Team should train with the Tactical Team. Doing so enhances each team's ability to function effectively, by being able to anticipate each other's actions. It is a given that tactical and negotiation teams operate side by side. If one does not work, the other will. Both teams can enhance the effectiveness of the other through an exchange of vital information. To perfect this concept, interaction between the two teams should be encouraged. Some agencies take this to the extreme and actually combine both teams into one large team, composed of negotiators and tactical team members. This concept is workable, but debated among professionals.

COMMAND

If there is one, single team commander over both teams, that individual must be capable of understanding and in fact, embracing both methods of terminating an incident, tactically and through negotiations. This, in itself, may be difficult due to the fact of individuals tending to favor one method or the other. However, someone at command level must be able, after input from both the negotiations and tactical teams, to make a decision regarding how the situation will ultimately be handled.

PERFECTING THE TEAM

Once a functioning Hostage Team is operational, it is up to the team members to maintain their effectiveness. This is most certainly accomplished in conjunction with administrators, managers and, supervisors. As stated previously, a total buy-in from all levels is essential when it comes to specialized teams. Training classes must be sought out and utilized in order to obtain and perfect negotiating techniques and methods. The FBI offers hostage negotiating training at no cost to local law enforcement agencies while, numerous other providers throughout the nation also offer excellent training in this area. No matter what road you chose to travel in acquiring the necessary training, just make sure that the training is consistent with your specific policies and procedures, is fully documented and is provided by reputable instructors.

More than anything, make sure that you do receive some type of formal training. This above all, will cover most liability issues. Remember that training may be expensive, but not when compared to a lawsuit.

CHAPTER 7 REVIEW QUESTIONS

1. In creating a Hostage Negotiation Team, the most important aspect is _____.

   • The selection process

2. True or False - Ideally, Hostage Teams should encompass both male and female members, a wide age group and, a variety of ethnic backgrounds.

   • True

3. After a formal Hostage Negotiation Team is organized, training becomes essential. The first topic that should be covered is _____.

   • Crisis Intervention

4. Scenario training is a very effective method to better the skill of negotiators. If possible, the Negotiating Team should train with the _____ in order to coordinate their efforts during an actual incident.

   • Tactical Team or SWAT Team

5. True or False - To make the Hostage Team an effective and essential part of any law enforcement agency, total buy-in from all levels must be obtained.

   • True

ROLE OF NEGOTIATOR

Establishing personal contact with the hostage taker is a critical goal of the negotiator. Immediately after contact has been made, information such as the individual's name, age, sex, race and mental status, if available, will all serve to clarify the nature of the hostage situation. Any questioning beyond the information gathering stage needs to become open ended, requiring narrative rather than "Yes" or "No" responses from the hostage taker. It is hoped that by structuring the interaction in this way, the perpetrator will be encouraged to talk about his feelings, rather than impulsively act on them.

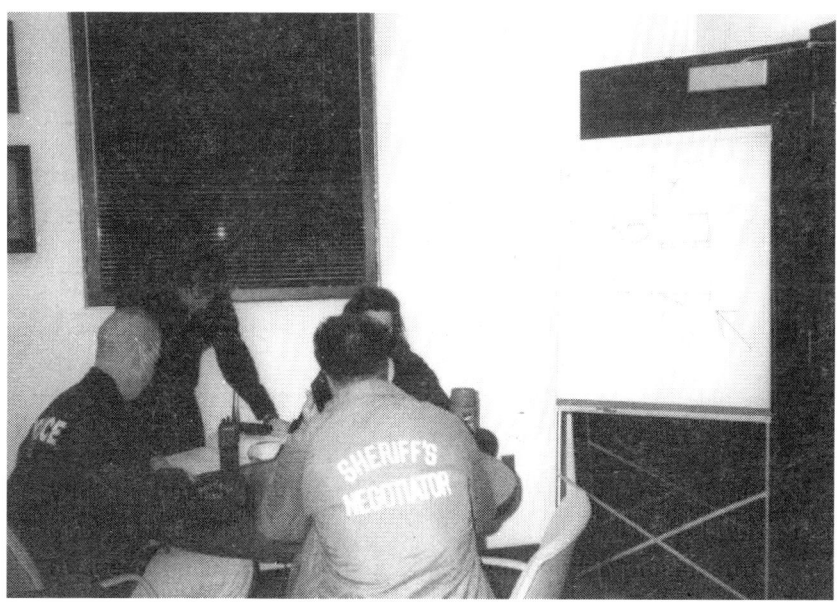

Hostage Team Members establishing contact with the hostage taker by phone. Their job is to introduce a climate of concern and compromise.

You should identify yourself by name, and address the offender in the manner he desires. The sooner this can be done the sooner a helpful and problem solving relationship can be established. Once a minimal relationship has been initiated, you can begin to communicate your awareness that a problem exists, that you want to understand the problem and that you are willing to help resolve it in a reasonable manner.

This problem solving atmosphere subtlety introduces a climate of concern and compromise. A statement to the effect that, "We" (the negotiator and the suspect), have got a problem that "We" can work out is a powerful message to the anxious, angry or confused offender. Providing the hostage taker with reassurances that a working relationship is possible and in everyone's best interests, introduces the possibility of further growth and expansion of the existing relationship, which involves bargaining.

BARGAINING

Bargaining is an essential component of successful hostage negotiation. Bargaining involves the exchanges arranged between the hostage taker and hostage negotiator, and is intended to promote a collaborative relationship between them. These exchanges may involve trading food and drink for a deadline extension or even for a sick, injured or frightened hostage. In any event, bargaining must be introduced early in the negotiation process, and be attached to the ultimate significance of each particular deal. The successful honoring of bargains made early on, sets a precedent for those to come.

MANAGEMENT OF TIME

The strategic use of time is an essential ingredient of hostage negotiation. It promotes the development of a number of processes that are related to the positive resolution of the incident, foremost of which is that with each passing hour the likelihood of violence decreases.

With the passage of time come the basic human needs for food, water, sleep and elimination. As these needs increase, so does the need for interaction and bargaining between the hostage taker and you. By accommodating these needs, an atmosphere of trust, understanding and compromise can begin to develop between the hostage taker and you. Anxiety also tends to decrease over a period of time, and most individuals begin to think more rationally and in general become less emotional.

Over time, many hostage taker's expectations and demands become more realistic. Ultimately, the successful use of time will serve to slow down the hostage taker and facilitate his reliance on you for information, supplies and support. Each additional minute allows for the gathering of more intelligence and better decision making on the part of the hostage negotiation team.

CHAPTER 8 REVIEW QUESTIONS

1. Striving for personal contact with the hostage taker is a critical goal. What should be done immediately after contact has been made with hostage taker?

   • Obtain information such as name, age, sex, race, and mental status, if available.

2. True or False - The management of time is usually related to the negative resolution of the incident.

   • False

3. True or False - The successful use of time will serve to slow down the hostage taker and facilitate his reliance on you for information.

   • True

HOSTAGE TEAM GUIDELINES

The negotiation process is an involved, technical one that requires the best possible effort from responding units. For this reason, agencies are advised to select and designate specific personnel to play the role of Hostage Team members. The members of this team form the nucleus of a planned, effective response to a critical incident. With this in mind, it becomes essential to form a basis for team member selection and general team set-up.

Team members should be selected from a list of volunteer officers, who will serve in this capacity while continuing to perform their regular full-time duties. In other words when critical incident occurs, team members are called in or pulled from their regular assignment to perform their roles on the team. At the very least, an oral interview should be conducted with each volunteer in order to select the most qualified. Many agencies require a psychological test of each prospective volunteer prior to selection. The primary goal is to select individuals who exhibit empathic and sensitive personalities, demonstrating the ability to intervene successfully in crisis situations. Generally speaking, the team should reflect the makeup of the surrounding community, mirroring the local nationality, ethnicity and language spoken, and should include both male and female officers.

Basic duties are assigned to each member of the Hostage Team, with the understanding that each member is cross-trained so they may perform each duty when and if necessary. The following is a list of specific tasks which may be assigned to a typical team:

Hostage Team Commander
Is responsible for all actions taken by the team. They assign specific roles to members at the scene of an incident and interact with Command Personnel in the Command Post.

Assistant Team Commander

Assumes the command of the team when the Commander is not present. They may fill in as needed if there are vacant positions within the team structure and assists in the set-up of all of the team equipment.

Primary Negotiator

Speaks directly to the hostage taker and therefore, functions as the direct line from that suspect to a successful outcome of the incident.

Back-Up Negotiator

Fills in for the Primary Negotiator, if necessary. They take notes during the conversation so that if called upon to take the Primary's place, they are aware of every issue that has been discussed and or negotiated.

Intelligence Officer

Organizes all incoming information and presents it to the team in an orderly, factual manner. They conduct interviews of witnesses and released hostages, relaying pertinent information to those in charge and to the team members. Quite often, due to the amount of work, this position is usually filled by more that one individual.

Tactical Liaison Officer

Maintains communications with the Tactical Team (SWAT) and relates this information to the Hostage Team. By doing this, efforts of both teams remain coordinated and in turn are directed toward a common goal. By maintaining solid communications between negotiators and tactical personnel, mistakes and misinterpretations are kept to a minimum.

All of the above positions may or may not be filled at every critical incident however, at a minimum, a Primary and Back-up Negotiator is a necessity. Depending upon the size and philosophy of your particular agency, the Hostage Negotiation Team may either be separate from the Tactical Team or part of that team. By having each team designed as a separate entity, Command Staff receives input from two different Team Commanders thus, affording them information and recommendations from two different outlooks. It then becomes the responsibility of the Command Staff to weigh the input and determine the best option to employ. If both teams are placed under one Commander, Command Staff receives a recommendation from that individual only. This in and of itself, may cause a problem unless the single Team Commander is adept at both tactical and negotiation methods. In other words, that individual must be comfortable in employing either solution to the crisis, when and where necessary.

Upon the arrival of the Hostage Negotiation Team at the scene of a critical incident, the initial set-up of personnel and equipment must begin as soon as possible. Ideally, the team should be placed in a location separate from the immediate area of the Command Post. This allows the team members to perform their duties apart from the major activity consistent with the functions of the Command Staff. The Hostage Team/Tactical Team Commander should report directly to the Command Post to obtain necessary information regarding the incident and in turn, pass this on to the team members.

Hostage Team Members at scene of critical incident.
The team is the link between the critical incident and a successful conclusion.

While the above is taking place, the team members should set-up and test any and all special equipment which may be employed during the incident. Throw-phones, loud speakers, cameras, microphones, bullhorns, tape recorders, etc. should be prepared and ready for employment when needed. Specific assignments should be designated and all preliminary intelligence should be reviewed. All of the interaction between the Hostage Team and the Command Post should be handled through the Hostage/Tactical Team Commander thereby, keeping the hectic activity in the Command Post as far from the Hostage Team negotiation process as possible.

Initially, the Hostage Team should begin obtaining information from as many sources that are available. Witnesses, released hostages, the first officer on the scene, etc. must all be debriefed in an effort to discover the basic status of the incident and in turn, the appropriate response. In short, the Hostage Team becomes the link between the critical incident and a successful conclusion.

CHAPTER 9 REVIEW QUESTIONS

1. How should hostage teams members be selected?

   • From a list of volunteers

2. Who is responsible for all actions taken by the team?

   • Hostage Team Commander

3. Who speaks directly to the hostage taker?

   • Primary Negotiator

4. True or False - Basic duties are assigned to team members with the understanding that each member is crossed trained so they may perform each duty when and if necessary.

   • True

5. True or False - By maintaining solid communication between negotiator and tactical personnel, mistakes and misinterpretations are kept to a minimum.

   • True

HOSTAGE NEGOTIATIONS
PROCEDURES AND PRINCIPLES

Since the 1970's the concept of hostage negotiations has been an acceptable and effective method of handling crisis situations. The following ideals and prescripts are offered to you in an attempt to cover some of the basic issues which may assist in the performance of Hostage Negotiation Teams and their endeavor to reach their ultimate goal, the successful termination of an incident.

Information Gathering

Gather Information about the Suspect as quickly as possible, you should attempt to obtain as much information regarding the suspect and his personality. In doing so, you will stand a better chance of resolving the incident. Specific probing questions should be reduced to a form, which is carried by the Hostage Team members and utilized in this type of situation. Questions may include, but certainly not be limited to:

- Name, age, race
- Physical condition and whether the suspect is under medication and if so, has possibly failed to take it.
- Aggression potential
- Criminal record
- Degree of rationality
- Present motivation
- Politics
- Purpose of the hostage taking
- Available weapons

Once knowing who the suspect is and his basic personality traits, negotiation tactics may be implemented accordingly.

Establish a Problem Solving Climate

While interacting with the suspect, you must continually communicate that you truly understand his points, that you truly desire to work with him in an attempt to find a solution to this incident and, that you actually are willing to compromise in attaining that solution. In effect, what this means is that you will lead the suspect to believe that together, you can and indeed will, reach an acceptable solution. In short, focus on defeating the problem at hand, not on defeating each other.

Build Trust

The most important aspect to reach in the negotiation process is that of building and reaching a level of trust of the negotiator by the suspect. Once this feeling of trust is obtained, the negotiator has "Won" the situation. This means that when the suspect is able to actually trust the negotiator, progress will be realized almost immediately and this progress will hopefully result in a successful outcome of the incident. The basic issue then is how do you build this trust? Simply put, you continually suggest to the suspect that they can indeed trust you. The longer the incident lasts, the more you are able to influence the suspect that his trust in you is valid. You will then find that some point in the negotiations, the suspect may simply state, "I think I can trust you."

Avoid Forcing a Climate

Some negotiators feel a need to make the suspect conform to the negotiator's plan of action. This in turn, places the incident into a "Win-Lose" concept. If you as the negotiator, take an aggressive stance in this type of situation you may find yourself in a position where the hostages are threatened. The suspect may feel a need to exhibit a show of force in an attempt to prove is in control. Naturally, this is the worst case situation for you to be confronted with and in turn, should be avoided at all costs.

Attempt to Calm the Suspect

Through the use of carefully chosen words, your tone of voice and, if visible to the suspect, your facial expressions, you can make it clear that you, the negotiator, are working in a calm and controlled manner. This will ease the tension levels and promote better communication. Speak in a slow and deliberate tone, demonstrating that everything is under control from your end, and a tactical response is not imminent. The suspect's reaction to this may be reflected in their interaction with the negotiator. In other words, they may attempt to model themselves after the negotiator and maintain a calm manner during the negotiating process. Tell the suspect that, "Together, we can work this out." "We can take this one step at a time," or "I know we can find a solution to this."

Attempt to Distract the Suspect from the Problem

At times, an effective method of calming a suspect is by diverting their attention away from the original cause of the problem. Asking questions, which are not directly related to the problem itself, can effectively do this. Additionally, you may discuss personal or other issues, which have no direct relevance to the incident, in an effort to distract the suspect and in turn, calm the situation.

These issues may range from particulars regarding his family to vacations he may have recently taken. For example, if he mentions a problem with his brother, you may reply that you have had a similar problem with your brother. If he had visited a particular vacation resort, you may have also. Talk about it. The main concept is to help create a personal relationship with the suspect, to build a belief that you are interested in his life above and beyond the incident that you are both involved in.

Stall For Time

Generally speaking, the longer a hostage situation goes, the better it is for the negotiator. Time allows the suspect to vent their emotions and draw closer to the negotiator thus, building rapport and nurturing trust. As time continues to move on, tactical units have a chance to review alternatives and develop strategies to address the situation. These units can actually practice entry methods so that when called upon to employ a tactical entry into the suspect's location, their practiced methods enhances their probability of success. Time also increases the basic needs of the suspect. The need for food, water, sleep, etc. can and often does play a large role in the negotiation process.

Do Not Argue With or Provoke the Suspect

Any type of crisis situation is an emotional experience for all those involved. As difficult as it may be, do not become overly aggressive or offensive. Now is not the time to reject all of the suspect's demands outright. Try not to talk down to them in an attempt to humiliate the suspect and show them the futility of their actions. Show a level of warmth toward the suspect, always trying to build rapport and trust. This may be particularly difficult for the negotiator if the suspect has done some repulsive deed.

Help the Suspect Save Face

You, as the negotiator, are in a position to lead the suspect toward an outcome that is acceptable to law enforcement while at the same time, lead them into believing that they are not losing. With this in mind, you allow the suspect to maintain a sense of dignity and foster better rapport. If on the other hand, you publicly defeat or humiliate the suspect, they may respond with a show of violent behavior.

Actively Listen to the Suspect

When interacting with the suspect listen to what they are saying and HOW it is being said. Tone of voice may actually indicate something completely different than what is being said. At times, restate the suspect's words; i.e., paraphrase showing your interest, attention and general understanding of their concerns. You may actually appear to agree in part with the suspect's viewpoint, especially early in the negotiation process. This will help later by decreasing his resistance to certain ideas that you may present.

Deal With Small Issues First

During the negotiations, small, easier to settle items may present themselves. Take this opportunity to work those out and again, building trust and rapport. Items and issues such as food, cigarettes and meeting the media after the incident is over are things, which can be agreed upon, ultimately leading to a successful outcome of the situation. When working on these issues, do not give in immediately. Formulate the idea that you are working hard to obtain any and all desired items. This will show the suspect that your are actually working in their best interest, knowing all of the time that you are building a foundation to end the incident on your terms.

Present Both Sides of the Argument

While speaking with the suspect, show them that you are able to discuss their side of the issue while still presenting your viewpoint. This will show that your are objective and reasonable. In short, by doing this you actually increase your persuasiveness.

Point Out Similarities

Continuing in the attempt to build rapport and trust, you can discuss any similarity between you and the suspect. Are you the same age, nationality, or race. Do you have a family or children, etc? Try to build on these issues and at times, talk about them during the negotiation process. By speaking about similarities, you can branch out to other issues and find a meeting point.

Request Delayed Compliance

If you are involved in issues that are difficult to address and gain acceptance, tell the suspect that they do not have to make a decision now. Ask the suspect to think about the issue or proposal and just keep his mind open. You may find that the suspect will still never agree however, this concept may add time to the process.

Keep Hope Alive

During the entire incident, your job is to keep the suspect believing that they have hope of "winning." Never make the mistake of creating an atmosphere that would lead the suspect to believe that they have nothing to lose if they injure or kill a hostage.

Ask the Suspect to Surrender

Because we tend to become deeply involved in crisis incidents, the obvious is often overlooked. We become so engrossed in

"Procedure" that we forget to as the one, most important question, "Will you cease what you are doing, come out and meet with me?" The answer may be, "Yes." If this is the case, the incident is over before it actually begins. There have been occasions where all responding units performed outstandingly, setting up perimeters, a command post, staging area, etc., and only after all this had been accomplished, hours into the negotiation process was this question asked and in turn, agreed upon. By doing this early on in the incident, time, money and problems could be held to a minimum.

Your primary responsibility in a hostage/crisis incident is the safe release of the hostages. If this can be accomplished through a negotiation that is best however, if not, a tactical response will be necessary. In short, negotiations do not always succeed making it not the only way but the preferred way to end a crisis situation.

INTERACTION DIALOG

Privacy

Unlike the crowded, tense and noisy locations used by movie negotiators, actual hostage negotiators function best in a private setting. Of course situations dictate the amount of privacy available. It's much more comfortable to engage in a life or death dialog with a hostage without a lot of distracting people and activity around.

However, it's absolutely paramount that the backup negotiator listens in on the line so if the primary negotiator is unable to continue, the backup can seamlessly step in and continue, armed with all the available information.

Subterfuge

Occasionally, the negotiator will decide to tell a "story" such as: "My wife left me too, I know just how you feel." This risky tactic might create an empathetic bond with the hostage taker, however, they might see through the ruse and trust may be lost. "Stories" should be used with great care.

A "lie" may be told to the hostage taker as a means of stalling for time. For example, keeping his mind busy waiting for the "helicopter to arrive" may give the tactical team time to set up. Lies many times have consequences, so they must be used judiciously. A "lie sheet" is used to record what has been told to the hostage taker. This enables the backup negotiator to have an accurate account of the proceedings should they need to step in.

WORDS AND PHRASES

Each negotiator will have a manner of speaking and communicating that is unique to the individual. However, the following words and phrases have worked well in past situations:

- First I would like to get to know you better.

- Could you tell me about it?

- I would like to hear your side.

- Could you share that with me?

- I guess that's pretty important to you.

- That's interesting.

- I see.

- Is that so?

- I am here to help.

- Together, we can work this out.

Trigger Words

The following words are considered "trigger words" and may raise the anxiety level in the hostage or even provoke him to act.

- Gun

- Kill

- Shoot

Things to Do

When engaged in a dialog with a hostage taker, the negotiator should:

- Control your voice (slow down, use a low voice and be polite)

- Never give the impression of being a decision-maker

- Share information with secondary negotiator

- Show no concern for the hostage

- Not speak while the perpetrator is talking

- Offer nothing - wait until the hostage taker asks

- Not acknowledge deadlines

- Write everything related to demands down

- Never identify yourself by "rank"

- Maintain the "lie sheet"

CHAPTER 10 REVIEW QUESTIONS

1. What is the most important aspect to reach in the negotiation process?

    • Building and reaching a level of trust of the negotiator by the hostage taker.

2. Why is stalling for time a good procedure to use?

    • The longer a hostage situation goes, the better it is for the negotiator. Time allows hostage takers to vent their emotions and draw closer to the negotiator.

3. True or False - You, as the negotiator, are in a position to lead the suspect toward an outcome that is acceptable to law enforcement while at the same time, lead them into believing that they are not losing.

    • True

4. True or False - While speaking with the hostage taker, let them know that you are not going to discuss their side of the issue, only your viewpoint.

    • False

5. True or False - During the entire incident, your job is to keep the hostage taker believing that they have hope of "winning."

    • True

THE DISTURBED HOSTAGE TAKER & THE NEGOTIATOR

DIAGNOSTIC CATEGORIES

We have found the majority of emotionally disturbed hostage takers fall into one of four diagnostic categories:

1. Paranoid Schizophrenic type

2. Bipolar Disorder, or Manic-depressive type, with psychotic features

3. Antisocial Personality Disorder

4. Inadequate Personality

Before considering each of the above personality types, we would like to briefly discuss the skills and abilities we view as most relevant to negotiating with the emotionally disturbed offender. We consider a limited appreciation of abnormal psychology and a firm grasp of crisis intervention techniques as extremely important for this task. Your ability to identify an emotionally disturbed perpetrator will allow you to make adjustments in your strategy and seek appropriate consultation.

CRISIS INTERVENTION

Crisis intervention demands that you act quickly and decisively in assessing the crisis situation. Generally, intervening in a crisis like negotiation calls for the use of time to lessen anxiety, promote more reasonable thinking, facilitate the search for an alternative, and foster hope in the future. Your awareness of these principles will be useful throughout most negotiations, and is essential to negotiations with the emotionally disturbed suspect.

When negotiating with the emotionally disturbed hostage taker, the negotiator should have a limited appreciation of abnormal psychology and a firm grasp of crisis intervention techniques.

THE PARANOID SCHIZOPHRENIC HOSTAGE TAKER

The paranoid schizophrenic has been misrepresented both in the popular press and in criminal justice literature. While this individual has the potential for being extremely disorganized or outwardly psychotic, it has been the intact presentation that has led to "misdiagnosis" by authorities, mental health professionals and hostage negotiators alike. This individual's primary disturbance is his investment in, and reliance upon rigidly held beliefs, which are contrary to reality. These entrenched beliefs known as delusions are usually grandiose or persecutory in nature, and compel this individual to live with a distorted and exaggerated sense of importance, power, knowledge, or identity. At times, these delusions are accompanied by intrusive, mood congruent, auditory hallucinations. These hallucinations are commonly referred to as "hearing voices." When this individual does take hostages, he is often responding to an inner dialogue that drives him to act out his conflict with his family or friends.

In this situation, all the benefits and hazards associated with the Stockholm Syndrome (explained in Chap. 14) must be anticipated and planned for.

Making contact with an individual who is out of touch with reality is extremely challenging. When attempting to establish trust and rapport with this individual, it is important for you to accept distrust as an inevitable component of this relationship. In addition, the use of time in negotiating with this individual is extremely important.

With internal pressures so great this individual may have a powerful need to talk, to vent, and to relieve some of the pressures associated with his tremendous emotional burden. This process can be emotionally and physically draining for the hostage taker and ultimately work to your advantage and toward resolution of the incident. Throughout this process, you can be expected to experience a great deal of stress, since much of the content of this emotional discharge may be bizarre, shocking and upsetting.

To logically confront a delusional subject is a contradiction in terms, and a notion that is doomed to failure. A general understanding of schizophrenia and psychosis will help you avoid the temptations to problem solve, or confront the veracity of this offender's statements. Instead you must acknowledge the perpetrator's experiences and beliefs as being real for the offender, while understanding that he is not experiencing these things himself.

The role you must take on when dealing with the paranoid schizophrenic hostage taker is that of an interested listener. You must demonstrate this interest by asking questions about the tremendous pressures, which must accompany the perpetrator's beliefs and experiences. If after much time and dialogue the perpetrator appears to have calmed down, suggestions aimed at redirecting his efforts (not his ideas) may be introduced. At this point a safe resolution can often be achieved by incorporating some of the reformulated aspects of the offender's expressive demands into an honorable and safe solution.

Be aware that with the paranoid schizophrenic hostage taker, tactical assault may be necessary if:

- His mood and content of associations change abruptly

- He refuses further dialogue

- His agitation is increasing over time

- If one of his hostages has become a central figure in a prominent delusion

THE BIPOLAR OR MANIC DEPRESSIVE HOSTAGE TAKER

The psychologically depressed or bipolar manic depressive individual is the second most obviously disturbed hostage taker. This individual's depression has become so pervasive that it has led to a break with reality. Mood congruent delusions around past "sins," worthiness to live, and penance are common. This individual's potential for suicide is extremely high as is the potential for killing his hostages.

Like the schizophrenic hostage taker, the severely depressed perpetrator is most likely to hold members of his family hostage. His concerns often center around the decision of whether or not to allow himself and his family to continue living in such a decadent world. If you were to encounter this offender face to face, you would observe all the vegetative signs of depression including slow and labored speech, restlessness, poor concentration and heavy posture.

Negotiations with this subject are extremely tenuous. They must proceed astride this hostage taker's inhibited pace of physical and psychological functioning. His thoughts are fixed on themes of worthlessness, sinfulness, and extreme guilt.

Again, as when dealing with any delusion situation, you must constantly be aware not to confront or challenge these beliefs directly. In this type of negotiation, this mistake is most likely to take the form of exhortation or other forms of "cheering up." Such an intervention may lead to a break in the empathic bond that had developed to that point and result in the termination of negotiations and to eventual tragedy. A decrease in agitation and gradual improvement over a period of hours is the most hopeful sign in this hostage situation. After some time and dialogue, you can begin to work toward the expansion of the existing relationship. This expansion can be the natural outgrowth of concerns expressed earlier in the negotiations.

Contrary to popular belief, introducing the subject to the topic of suicide will not put a novel thought into the head of an individual who believes the world is a horrible and wicked place. This type of remark tends to underscore for the hostage taker the degree of understanding you have developed for him and his problems. Once a discussion of suicide occurs, it often signals a de-escalation of the crisis. It allows for the use of clarification, a therapeutic technique where the negotiator reflects back to the offender a clearer, less distorted picture of the confusing thoughts and feelings he has been experiencing. Once the level of interaction between you and the depressed hostage taker has reached this point, surrender is often near.

Through the introduction and discussion of emotionally taxing issues, this offender is often physically exhausted. Allowing time and fatigue to run their course, some of these negotiations have been reported to end with the hostage taker simply curling up in a ball and falling asleep.

THE ANTISOCIAL HOSTAGE TAKER

Neither the antisocial or inadequate personality suffer from delusions or hallucinations, instead, they suffer from personality disorders. A personality disorder is believed to be present when personality traits are inflexible and unadaptive and cause significant impairment in social or occupational functioning. Antisocial personality individuals are basically unsocialized and whose behavior pattern brings them repeatedly into conflict with society.

They are incapable of significant loyalty to individuals, groups, or social values. They are generally grossly selfish, callous, irresponsible, impulsive, and unable to feel guilt or to learn from experience or punishment.

You can begin to formulate the difficulties inherent in negotiating with the antisocial hostage taker. This individual can be encountered in a jewelry store, bank, jail or his home. In terms of the nature of his demands, the antisocial hostage taker will typically make both expressive and instrumental demands. He will use the hostage taking incident for both personal gain and psychological satisfaction.

Thus, money and transportation may be demanded in such a way as to maximize the embarrassment or humiliation of his hostages and law enforcement officials. As this offender is no stranger to conflict, he is likely to respond to you as he would to any authority figure and anger, contempt and distrust.

Often the experienced and inexperienced negotiator alike will have a strong and negative reaction to the interpersonal response this perpetrator draws from negotiators. First, it is immediate; second, it often takes place outside the full awareness of the negotiator; and third, it can lead to an escalating cycle of unproductive and hostile exchanges between the hostage taker and you the negotiator. Relying on the psychological consultant and other members of the negotiation team will allow you to avoid falling into this dangerous interaction pattern.

It is paradoxical that while cut off from his own emotions, the antisocial offender is keenly aware of the emotional experience of those around him. If you attempt to build a warm and trusting relationship with this individual you may be met by the derision discussed above or worse, with feigned emotional sincerity.

In the latter case, you may be manipulated into planning a negotiation strategy around a relationship, which exists in his mind alone. With the antisocial hostage taker, it is extremely unlikely that the Stockholm Syndrome will work to the advantage of the negotiation team. Instead, this individual will employ his charm and considerable intelligence to choreograph his victim's thoughts and emotions to his own ends. At the same time, he will stand ready, willing and able to dispatch whatever degree of violence needed to maintain control and secure his demands.

Through his diminished capacity to tolerate frustration or boredom, the antisocial hostage taker significantly limits your use of stalling for time. As he becomes frustrated, angry or bored he may be tempted to turn his attention to his hostages. At this point you must assert yourself and redirect the hostage taker's attention. Such straight forward advice as, "Hey Tom, all you tried to do was take some money - so far nobody has been hurt - why don't we keep it that way" may be useful.

This type of advice makes the antisocial hostage taker aware that keeping the hostages in good physical condition if nothing else, is in his own best interest. Further, you must liberally employ bargaining as a strategy. You must push to get something in return for something provided. Doing favors for the antisocial offender does not necessarily build rapport or gratitude.

Failure to successfully resolve negotiations with the antisocial hostage taker is often the result of this individual's emotional volatility. Often through an impulsive or violent act negotiations are abruptly broken off. The individual has "decided" to shoot his way out, chance an escape, or act out his frustration and loss of control by injuring or attempting to take the lives of his hostages. By reasserting his need for control in this manner, the antisocial hostage taker will also have forced the hand of law enforcement officials. As a result, tactical assault will be necessary.

THE INADEQUATE PERSONALITY HOSTAGE TAKER

Though no longer a formal diagnostic category, the inadequate personality remains a useful typology for law enforcement officials. This offender has been described as immature, submissive and passive aggressive in his interpersonal relations and suffering from instability in his mood and behavior.

The inadequate personality type is ineffectual in his ability to cope with most social, emotional or physical stresses. He suffers from bouts of depression and feels completely dependent upon others to rescuer him from these depressive episodes. Frustration in any form is experiences as rejection and initiates a downward spiral of self-doubt and despair. Self-destructive behavior aimed toward reestablishing dependent and pathological relationships will often parallel such moods.

Taking hostages for this individual often occurs during the course of a bungled crime. Despite this criminal context, this hostage taker is seen as operating in order to meet some unconscious or unarticulated psychological need. The commission of a crime by this offender is often a thinly veiled attempt to communicate to parents, ex-lovers or co-workers. After the initial crime has been foiled, the act of taking hostages is often a desperate attempt to stave off yet another personal failure.

This hostage taker is not psychotic and despite his intense manner, is quite amenable to the negotiation process. The Stockholm Syndrome will serve to protect hostages in incidents involving the inadequate personality. However, the possibility exists that complications in the negotiations may arise due to hostages responding positively to this subject.

With this potential in mind, successful negotiations with this hostage taker are anchored in the development of an uncritical, understanding and empathic relationship between you and the perpetrator. Negotiators are often struck by the juvenile nature of his threats and demands.

Through the use of time and bargaining, a strong bond between you and this offender develops. Active use of crisis intervention techniques will serve to solidify this relationship. This offender can benefit from a discussion of his alternative solutions. Since he is not psychotic, and his character is anchored around dependency, he will often gravitate to the strong and supportive relationship provided by you. After a period of time it will become evident that if you can help this individual "save face" a successful outcome will result. Often, due to the power of the relationship, surrendered will occur if this hostage taker believes he has proven himself to you.

The special challenge that the inadequate personality holds for the negotiator is his high potential for suicide. This offender is much more likely to kill himself than other non-psychotic hostage takers. During the course of negotiations, this perpetrator will grow increasingly aware that he is in over his head, that he is both unwilling and unable to kill his hostages, and that he has failed again. What makes this particularly dangerous is that this individual has been reported to set up situations in which the police must shoot him. Such an incident is likely to involve the hostage taker specifically disobeying an agreed upon condition of surrender.

In some instances you may be alerted to this covert agenda by noting that the hostage taker has begun to make special arrangements or preparations just prior to his surrender. If you sense that suicide is the primary motive behind surrender, you should share those concerns with the hostage taker. An empathic reexamination of options will often facilitate a safe resolution of this incident.

Negotiation with emotionally disturbed hostage takers is likely to be a more frequently experienced, demanding and challenging activity. It has been our intention to outline the challenges and underscore the opportunities that are a part of negotiating with these individuals. It was our hope to share our belief that successful hostage negotiation with the emotionally disturbed offender combines basic negotiation strategies with specific psychological skills and abilities. While we are not advocating extensive changes in negotiator training or qualifications, we do believe that a degree of psychological sophistication can help in identifying and managing the emotionally disturbed hostage taker.

CHAPTER 11 REVIEW QUESTIONS

1. Why is a general understanding of schizophrenia and psychosis important?

   - It will help you avoid the temptation to problem solve, or confront the veracity of this offender's statement. Instead you must acknowledge the schizophrenic hostage taker's experiences and beliefs as being real. to him, while understanding that he is not experiencing these things himself.

2. What is your role when dealing with the paranoid schizophrenic?

   - Be an interested listener. Demonstrate this interest by asking questions about the tremendous pressures, that accompany the schizophrenic's beliefs and experiences.

3. True or False - The psychologically depressed or bipolar manic depressive individual is the second most obviously disturbed hostage taker.

   - True

4. True or False - Neither the antisocial or inadequate personality suffer from personality disorders, they suffer from delusions or hallucinations instead.

   - False

5. True or False - Taking hostages for the inadequate personality hostage taker often occurs during the course of a bungled crime.

   - True

INTERACTING WITH EXTREMISTS/TERRORISTS

Today's world is more complicated and interwoven than ever before in history. We are being confronted on all levels with vast differences of deep-seated beliefs, such as political doctrine, matters of life and death or religious outlook. In the recent past, our nation has faced the actions of the Left Wing, Right Wing, various militias, the onslaught of inner city gangs, religious zealots and other "Patriots," to name a few. Locations such as Ruby Ridge, Waco, and Oklahoma City will forever be etched into out memories as horrendous situations, which resulted in major injuries and death. These types of situations bring us face to face with individuals who do not view the world and its people in the same light as the majority of our population. In turn, law enforcement often times is called upon to intervene and attempt to neutralize unacceptable situations.

Extremists / Terrorists are opportunists seeking an audience.

WHO ARE THEY?

A large portion of hostage takers can be identified as being sociopathic individuals who will do anything to accomplish their planned agenda. Extremists and terrorists can be view in a similar light. For them, the end justifies the means. As far as the extremists are concerned, the better and more favorable the press coverage is, the better the cause is served. In some instances, media coverage may be the primary reason for the incident to have occurred in the first place.

The Radical Rights groups are primarily concerned with their First, Second and Fourteenth Amendment rights. Groups such as the "Skinheads" rely on their interpretation of past history (World War II and Adolph Hitler) to foster their present day beliefs.

These individuals often state their freedom of speech rights and in so doing, express themselves accordingly. We must understand that their right of expression does not allow them to become violent and when or if they do, society must step in and take control.

Our society in general has been conditioned to view the extremist/terrorist as being some type of superman and freedom fighter. He is neither. The movie industry has developed a certain inaccurate persona regarding the terrorist. He is depicted as having a strong support system and excellent tactics, all of which seem to indicate that the terrorist is highly committed to his cause, highly trained and an expert in his field.

Analyzing past incidents, we many times find just the opposite. From terrorists who did not know how or what to negotiate for, to terrorists who actually believed that a commercial airliner was able to land in water, float and then be driven onto land. We have found that these individuals were indeed not "Supermen." In short, we must not overestimate the abilities of these groups however, at the same time we must acknowledge the very real danger posed by them.

OUR RESPONSE

When viewing incidents, which involve extremists/terrorists, many individuals in the field of negotiations may feel it necessary to change long-standing, proven tactics and negotiation practices. This however, should not be the case. The techniques, which have been proven to work with other types of hostage takers, will also work with this type of hostage taker.

The specific concerns and issues present in, for example, a politically motivated hostage incident may weigh heavily in the tactics and interaction between the suspect and the negotiator; however, the basic negotiating principle remains the same. The negotiating team must determine the facts, assess all the information, determine the potential for violence from the suspect, find out the suspect's motive and demands and finally, make recommendations to the incident commander. As always, the process may remain the same while the factors and issues may vary from incident to incident.

Extremists/Terrorists all depend upon outside elements, not only for training and equipment, but also for moral and emotional backing. This becomes increasingly more important during a prolonged incident. As time wears on, total commitment to the "Cause" may wane, based upon the days or weeks the subject is physically away from their support system. This factor should be taken into account because it plays an important role in the negotiation process. As emotional and physical exhaustion sets in, the subject may be more open to the proposals offered by the negotiator. Their willingness to do whatever may have been planned in the beginning may indeed change as the incident continues; in short, what they were willing to die for at the start, may not be an issue they are willing to die for towards the end.

THIRD PARTY INTERVENTION

Throughout the history of hostage negotiations, the use of a third party (non-law enforcement personnel), has been both successful and unsuccessful in attaining a peaceful solution to an incident.

These individuals, whether they are clergy, interpreters, medical doctors or significant others, may offer a viable alternative for the negotiator to utilize in attempting to find a solution to a volatile situation.

In dealing with extremists/terrorists, we must accept the basic concept of them viewing anyone associated with a government entity, i.e., law enforcement, as being the "Enemy." With this in mind, we are faced with the distinct possibility of working with an intermediary or third party. In recent years, our nation has been faced with a variety of incidents in which these third parties have contributed their time and expertise. When employing this tool, we must keep in mind that the responses we receive from the third party, especially if they are an interpreter, may be slanted, and based upon their personal feelings. For example, if the third party is a member of the clergy, as time goes on the possibility of theology taking a primary role in the conversation may come about. If the third party is being used as an interpreter we must also keep in mind what we, the negotiators, are quite possibly hearing is the interpretation of what the subject is actually saying. In effect there is some filtering of feedback from the subject, through the interpreter, to the negotiator. Based on this, interpretations should be double-checked prior to any action taken.

PRIOR PREPARATION

As in any crisis incident, the key to a successful solution rests in preparing for the event before it happens. This is especially the case in dealing with extremists/terrorists. If interpreters are to be used, we must make certain they are familiar with the techniques and goals of the negotiators. Additionally, we should be aware of possible problems, which may arise based upon various aspects of the interpreter or third party.

For example, is the interpreter completely fluent in the specific language and speaking the same dialect as the hostage taker? Is the third party used to talking with violent or aggressive individuals? Finally, is the third party's personal agenda the same as yours, or are they there for publicity or some other goal? All of these issues must be addressed prior to the incident occurring. With all the above concerns in mind, it becomes imperative to interview, select and train third party individuals, which you feel, may be called upon at the time of a crisis. This is, in and of itself, an extremely important issue. We cannot expect someone who has never come in contact with the criminal element to function well when faced with dealing with them in a crisis situation. Making the right selection and then training them thoroughly is the only method to employ, keeping in mind that the third party is not actually the negotiator, but only a tool to be used to attain your goal.

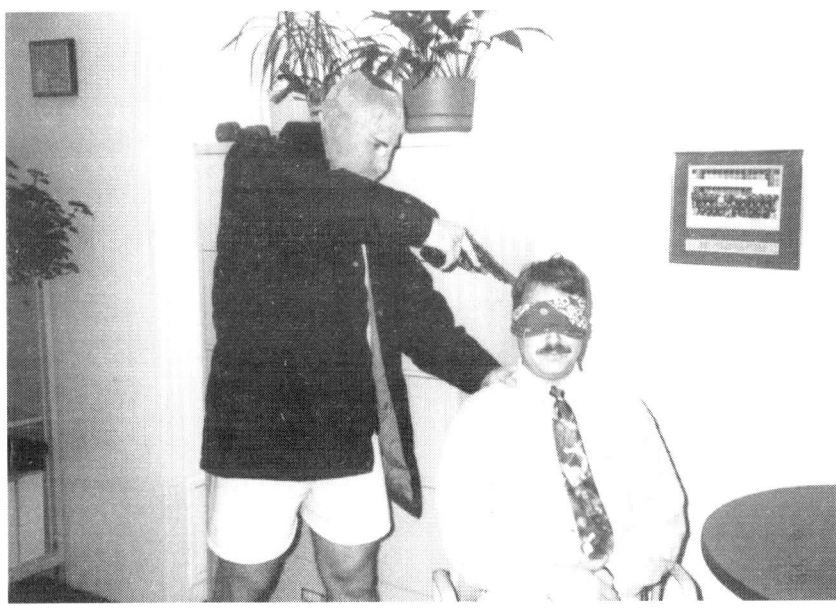

The Extremists / Terrorists will do anything to anybody
to accomplish their planned agenda.

CHAPTER 12 REVIEW QUESTIONS

1. True or False - A large number of hostage takers may be described as a sociopath.

    •   True

2. True or False - Extremists / Terrorists are usually highly trained "Supermen."

    •   False

3. True or False - When dealing with Extremists/Terrorists, basic hostage negotiation techniques should be used. These methods have been proven to be effective in these types of incidents.

    •   True

4. True or False - One type of third party, which may be called upon to assist in the negotiation process, may be a member of the clergy.

    •   True

5. True or False - It is extremely important to train any individual who may be called upon to assist in a crisis incident.

    •   True

LAW ENFORCEMENT & THE TERRORIST HOSTAGE TAKER

For the foreseeable future, terrorism, both domestic and international, will continue to be a major concern to U.S. Government and law enforcement agencies. Officers attending the FBI National Academy in Quantico, Virginia consistently voice concern over terrorism. Some officers have the impression that in a terrorist hostage incident, the crisis management approach would (or should) be substantially different from that in a criminal hostage incident. This is not the case.

Since the mid 1970's, the FBI has grouped hostage taking incidents into four broad categories:

1. The Terrorist

2. The Prison Situation

3 The Criminal

4. The Mentally Disturbed

State and local law enforcement officers at the FBI Academy have indicated that these four major categories are still commonly used by law enforcement agencies. There is also the consensus that the current set of negotiation strategies and tactics available to law enforcement provide viable alternatives from which to choose whatever the motivation for the taking of hostages.

Unfortunately, much of what is believed about terrorist conduct and behavior is derived from the media and the entertainment industry. Both the general population and the law enforcement community have come to accept the terrorist stereotype as accurately depicting personality traits, dedication, sophistication, commitment, and modus operandi.

All to often, the dramatic events surrounding a terrorist incident are misrepresented in fictional accounts or in media efforts aimed at recreating actual situations that have occurred.

Additionally, a brief news flash, broadcast during an ongoing terrorist siege, does not draw an accurate picture of a terrorist's total range of conduct and personality traits. Therefore, many of the expressed ideals regarding terrorists appear to be based upon incorrect perceptions.

THE TERRORIST HOSTAGE TAKER

The FBI defines terrorism as the unlawful use of force or violence against persons or property to intimidate or coerce a government, civilian population, or any segment thereof, in furtherance of political or social goals. One major difficulty in discussing the terrorist hostage taker is that the words "terrorist" and "terrorism" have been used by the media to such an extent that they are virtually useless as valid descriptive terms. They have become political terms with almost as many definitions as speakers have.

From the viewpoint of the crisis manager (i.e., the on-scene commander), does it help to distinguish a hostage taking as a terrorist act, separate from a criminal act? No, it does not. The label given the behavior does not change the act. In fact, the FBI now refers to such acts as "terrorist crimes" to underscore the fact that the motivation for the behavior does not change the criminality of such behavior. The emphasis here is not meant to imply a lesser risk but to stress that the act is, first and foremost, a violent crime in progress, regardless of the stated motivation of the hostage taker.

Labels and Tactics

Too often, those who are quick to point out that an act is a "terrorist incident" (or any other kind, for that matter), mistakenly confused the labeling with understanding. In this case, the label is one that is so subjective that it is meaningless. To describe an incident as only a "terrorist" event implies that all such events are similar. Even additional adjectives, such as "Palestinian" terrorist, fail to identify, for example, significant differences in motives, methods, and goals of various Palestinian factions, and of course, individual differences among the members themselves.

The use of a label is helpful only if the term is associated with essential elements that differentiate one set of behaviors from another. Perhaps a more descriptive term would be "planned political/religious" hostage taking, since this term does not have the emotional overtones currently attached to the word "terrorist." Such a term avoids the automatic and potentially misleading assumptions made when the word "terrorist" is used.

The essential question is, in confronting such an incident: Will your agency employ hostage negotiation/crisis management techniques that have been used successfully in a wide variety of hostage/barricade situations, or will those procedures be discarded? There exists a general assumption that this type of hostage incident, one that involves a terrorist, has a certain mystique about it. A feeling that the suspect is a brilliant mastermind, a superb tactician and an unbeatable foe. In reality, this is not the case. There are very few terrorists that would fall into this category and even fewer that would actually die for their cause. There are some, but not as many as one may think.

To our knowledge no scientific studies or analytical surveys exist that might serve to provide the basis for such a belief. In order to examine the validity of current crisis management/negotiation techniques in confronting such incidents, it is essential to separate common myth from factual knowledge.

THE LAW ENFORCEMENT RESPONSE

One question frequently asked by police officers is "How would you negotiate differently during a terrorist incident?" Once the distinction is made between kidnapping (where the location of subject and victim are typically unknown) and hostage taking (where the subject and victim are contained within a police perimeter), officers are surprised or perhaps disappointed to hear the answer. Basically, negotiation strategies and tactics for terrorist incidents are identical to those that would be used during any hostage or barricade incident, regardless of the political or religious backgrounds of the subjects.

Simply put, there are a number of strategies (and particular tactics to support each of these strategies) to choose from when negotiating with hostage takers that are contained and isolated. The fact that a particular group of subjects puts forth political or religious reasons for taking hostages does not call into play a conceptually different set of strategies. The negotiation team assesses the motives, demands, and behaviors of these hostage takers and makes recommendations to the on-scene commander as to the most appropriate strategy, drawn from the same set of possibilities as in any other hostage incident.

However, the specific factors they consider crucial to a particular incident, in all cases, depend on the circumstances of the hostage taker. For example, suppose a person claiming harassment and persecution by Federal authorities that are stealing thoughts from his mind took hostages in a public office building and threatened to kill the hostages unless the FBI stopped the persecution.

The same negotiation and tactical strategies used for common criminals is effective when negotiating with this type of individual.

The negotiation team would logically focus on the subject's medical history, seeking records of past treatment for mental disturbance, interviewing any mental health professional (MHP) who may have treated the subject, and perhaps using the MHP as a consultant.

On the other hand, if a group of subjects took the same hostages in the same building, but claimed to represent the "People's Holy Liberation Forces," the team would certainly value any information on the origins, beliefs, composition, and any previous actions by this group.

Knowledgeable sources on both the political and religious dogma of this group, as well as language experts, would be consulted and perhaps incorporated into the negotiation team. As you can see, the process of assessment and recommendation remains the same, but clearly the specific factors or issues that the team considers critical vary with each incident.

This is not to say that when a politically motivated incident occurs in the United States, there is not a greater amount of involvement by the higher levels of the U.S. Government, because there is. In fact, the desire of terrorists, both international and domestic, to focus media attention on their causes by staging attacks at locations or events of international interest, has made it necessary for governmental and law enforcement authorities to closely coordinate their preparations for special events. That involvement however does not call into play "better," or even different negotiation strategies or principles. The negotiation recommendations are simply reviewed by a longer chain of command.

Even as long as 12 years ago, John Stratton, author of The Terrorist Act of Hostage Taking: A view of Violence and the Perpetrator, stated that social, political or religious terrorists are the most difficult to deal with because of their commitment. However, he also pointed out that negotiation with some political or religious hostage takers has been successful.

When hostage takers plan to be surrounded, as in the takeover of a public building, the probability of a prolonged incident increases and the risk to the hostages is considered to be very high. However, notwithstanding the fact that such an incident was deliberately planned. The commitment of the hostage takers may not be a "total" commitment.

Post-incidents review of the behavior of some of the hostage takers in planned political incidents indicates that there may be a difference in being "willing" to die for a cause and in "wanting" to die for a cause. Once the subject has been away from a support system for days or weeks, and emotional or physical exhaustion sets in, that person may be more willing to accept the rationale presented by the negotiator.

POLITICAL/RELIGIOUS HOSTAGE TAKERS

Political hostage takers have been negotiated with effectively by stressing that their point has been made, their demands have been heard, their cause has been "aired" to the world, and therefore, killing hostages would only serve to discredit them and their cause in the eyes of the public. A.H. Miller, Author of Terrorism and Hostage Negotiations, concludes that police negotiating tactics that are most likely to succeed in planned political/religious situations, if the suspects are primarily interested in making a symbolic statement and obtaining publicity.

These negotiation tactics have in fact, been successful in resolving a number of political/religious hostage incidents in the United States and elsewhere. Even incidents that require a tactical resolution, such as the siege at the Iranian Embassy in London in April 1981 confirmed the appropriateness of these negotiating techniques.

The dangers posed by planned political/religious hostage-taking incidents should in no way be minimized. Rather, law enforcement should respond to these incidents in a manner that is consistent with the crisis management procedures that have been developed and validated through thousands of hostage situations worldwide.

If political/religious situations are accorded special status or are cause for law enforcement to ignore effective crisis management strategies, then law enforcement falls victim to the "terrorist mystique" that has allowed terrorist to become a potent weapon in recent years.

However, if a planned political/religious incident is not treated as a special case, and hostage takers instead are dealt with as any other high risk subject would be, then law enforcement will be better able to employ the professional skills learned through the lessons of past years.

CHAPTER 13 REVIEW QUESTIONS

1. True or False - Much of what is believed about terrorist conduct and behavior is derived from the media and the entertainment industry.

   • True

2. Who defined the following statement? Terrorism is the unlawful use of force or violence against persons or property to intimidate or coerce a government, civilian population, or any segment thereof, in furtherance of political or social goals.

   • FBI

3. True or False - It helps to distinguish a hostage taking as a terrorist act, separate from a criminal act.

   • False

4. True or False - Negotiation strategies and tactics for terrorist incidents are identical to those that would be used during any hostage or barricade incident, regardless of political or religious background of the hostage taker.

   • True

HOSTAGE SURVIVAL - JAIL OR PRISON EMPLOYEES

HOSTAGE! The word itself instills feelings of uncertainty, anxiety and fear in all individuals. Correctional officers are no different. Webster defines "hostage" as "one handed over to the enemy as security; one held by the enemy as a pledge for fulfillment of certain stated conditions." This is an unacceptable concept for many of us, but a concept nonetheless, that has become a fact of life. As a correctional officer, you perform under a large variety of stressful conditions. Some of you confront daily others not quite as often, and still others, hope never to confront. Being taken hostage falls into the last category. Many display what is called a "deny and repress" reaction; deny that the situation will ever occur and repress all thoughts concerning the situation. This naturally leads to little or no information gathering and worst of all, little or no training.

The past, as it often does, dictates the future. Hostage situations in correctional Institutions such as Attica, New York; Santa Fe, New Mexico; Oakdale, Louisiana; and Atlanta, Georgia; to name a few, made national headlines for their severity, duration and loss of life and property. We must remember that, unfortunately, correctional facilities have become somewhat of a gathering place for the worst and most violent among us. In other words, this setting is a microcosm of that which is worst in society.

INMATE MOTIVATION

Correctional Institutions may in and of themselves cause hostage situations to occur. Poor food, inadequate living conditions and unfair or biased treatment of inmates are but a few of the potential problems with which some Institutions are faced. Many inmates are often no more than desperate individuals who may have nothing to lose. They firmly believe that the only way to make their demands viable and worthy of some notice is to take a hostage and negotiate for a change of conditions.

Some changes are negotiable, i.e., Institutional food, amnesty for the hostage taken and their accomplices, more inmates input into the Institution's functions, etc. Whether demands are negotiable or not may depend upon strong policies or state law, both of which will vary from location to location. Whatever the case may be, we must be aware that a well-managed Institution is conducive to lessening potential inmate grievances and demands.

Generally speaking, approximately 18% of this country's population may be considered sociopathic, exhibiting some sort of antisocial personality traits. Approximately 45% of our inmate population fall into this category. These individuals usually have above average intelligence, but do not care about anything but themselves. These inmates will do anything they deem necessary to enhance their power. A sociopath has no qualms concerning the betrayal of fellow inmates. Their main objectives center on personal recognition, advancement and self-satisfaction. The hostage is literally a pawn in this game of self-gratification. Inmate's fear of one another or staff members may create undeserved feelings of the necessity of taking a hostage as a form of expression. The inmate attempts, in his own way, to make a statement as to his desperate and consuming fear for his safety. He grasps both figuratively and literally, at anything or anyone who may enhance his stand, and thereby increase his authority.

Dependent upon inmate population, various political groups may arise to challenge authority. May times, this challenge takes the form of a hostage taking incident. This type of zealot looks upon himself as a freedom fighter or a patriot rather that a criminal. In many cases, prison gang activity may also be viewed as a political statement. Gangs may now view hostage taking as a method to reach the media with their demands. Their cause, though unacceptable and irrational to the vast majority, is something they would fight for. For these individuals, hostage taking is a viable alternative.

In many instances, hostage situations in correctional settings center on one demand, Freedom. We must remember that many inmates found in our Institutions have extremely explosive personalities. These individuals tend to act out their emotions violently which, in many cases, is why they are incarcerated in the first place. If given a chance for freedom, these inmates will, and do, use hostages as bargaining chips. Life in a Correctional Institution may safely be viewed as monotonous and boring. Inmates have nothing but time on their hands and often look forward to any type of diversion. When they cannot adjust or cope with institutional life, rebellion takes place, which may culminate in a hostage situation.

BEING TAKEN HOSTAGE

Being taken hostage produces severe physical and emotional stress to your entire system. In any incident of this nature, there are some certainties, which have come to be expected. Correctional officers who are taken hostage will always be viewed as a threat by the hostage taker. Their mere presence will instill a concern in the hostage taker's mind of being overpowered. Your own handcuffs may be used to control you, as well as leg irons or empty cells, if available.

The key point here is control. Expect to be ordered about and moved from place to place, if possible. You must keep in mind that, at least according to the inmates, they have all the power; they have a hostage, they have you.

To an incarcerated inmate, a hostage incident may actually be the first time he had the power and opportunity to seek retaliation against those whom he believes he has reason to hate. Whether it is a particular officer or the system in general, there exists an extreme danger regarding the safety of hostages. A case in point is the Cuban uprising in Oakdale, Louisiana. The inmates protected various guards against violent and mentally ill Cubans. The above brings us to a point which all correctional officers should note. An institution's policies and procedures should be complied with from shift to shift and officer to officer. This effectively does away with individual officers treating various inmates differently. Grievances and complaints charging bias or discriminatory treatment by officers will be cut or eliminated, thereby decreasing the possibility of officers being labeled as lenient or overly strict. This ensures continuity of action, thus giving inmates a sense of stability and security in knowing that the Institution is operating as it should.

Every hostage situation is dangerous. As stated previously, hostages need not always be harmed, but at times inmates may feel a distinct necessity in injuring a hostage. This necessity may arise from a strong feeling of not being taken seriously by the administration. The hostage taker believes that he must make a strong statement to get attention and to be heard by those who are able to grant his wishes.

Many hostage incidents involve the use of the hostage as a shield. This seems to be a normal reaction by the hostage taker, especially when a face to face confrontation occurs. The hostage assumes the role of protection for the hostage taker, much as a bullet resistant vest. It is not uncommon for inmates to change clothing with hostage officers in order to increase their survival potential. Inmates are in constant fear of a sudden, overpowering assault by the Institution's staff. As in everyone, survival is an inmate's primary and strongest need. With this in mind, officers may be forced to exchange clothing with inmates to forestall and confuse a possible rescue attempt. The time it would take and the confusion involved for the institutional staff to identify inmates in officers' clothing would only work towards the benefit of the rebellious inmates.

Hostages have been used, in one way or another, to attempt to transmit information between the hostage taker and staff, or more precisely, the negotiator. In many instances, hostages have carried hand written notes to a drop off point, later to be picked up by a negotiator. Additionally, they have often been used to pick up food and other various items and return them to the hostage taker. Many times, the hostage taker as a means to verbally speak to the negotiator has utilized hostages. The hostage would be the one who is actually speaking to the negotiator on behalf of the hostage taker. In this type of situation, negotiations become extremely difficult because a third party is actually involved the hostage. We may be led to believe that this type of exchange would be mutually satisfying to both the hostage and the negotiator, but frankly, this may not be the case. What may arise is the negotiator becoming upset with the hostage, primarily based upon the behavior of the hostage during the incident.

During telephone communications with a negotiator, hostages have displayed a wide variety of reactions. The most common reaction is that of anger at the police and a general attitude that they are not doing anything to get the hostages safely out. This can be followed by a number of hostages actually verbally defending the hostage taker. The hostages may cry or panic, questioning the competence of the police and negotiator. The hostage may insult the negotiator while generally interfering with the negotiations and, lastly the hostage may request a hostage exchange.

The Stockholm Syndrome

Depending upon the duration of the incident, certain psychological events begin to transpire. The Stockholm Syndrome has been observed to occur worldwide whenever participants are thrown together in a highly stressful life and death situation, specifically a hostage incident. Simply stated, the Syndrome refers to a positive emotional bond between the hostage and the hostage taker that serves to promote the concept of "us against them." "Us" being the "victims" (hostage and hostage taker), while "them" are seen as the police (those on the outside who are attempting to settle the incident). As the time goes on, this emotional bond often becomes stronger and stronger.

Transference occurs somewhat along the same lines as the Stockholm Syndrome. Hostages given the time, feel as though the hostage taker's problem(s) are now theirs. Again, the "us against them" concept. Even a strong feeling such as fear, may turn from fear of the hostage taker to fear of the police. Hostages will come to believe that if only the police would leave or concede to the proposed demand(s), the entire incident would be over and everyone would be safe. Hostages may actually view the police as the major cause of the incident.

Many hostages are unprepared for this type of life and death situation, and therefore may feel as though the police (officers on the outside), who should help immediately are seemingly equally as helpless as the hostages. The hostage feels that the police have let him down by allowing this to happen in the first place. It should be noted that this positive emotional bonding often works in reverse, i.e., hostage to hostage taker. As time progresses, the hostage no longer is a faceless body, but instead becomes a human being, with feelings and emotions akin to the hostage taker. This fact alone has saved many hostages lives.

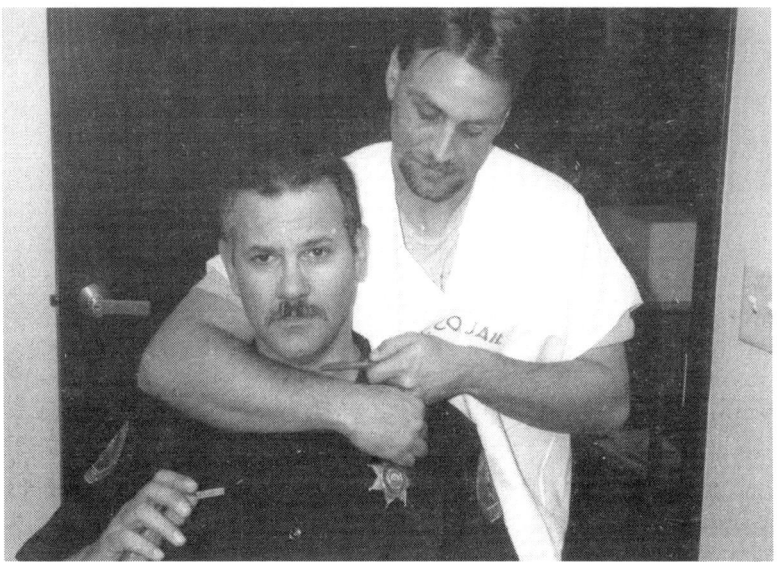

Don't try to be a "hero." Behave. Be the best hostage you can be.

Mental and Emotional Aspects of the Hostage Experience

The following are four general stages that a hostage goes through during an incident:

1. Denial

Denial is a basic but effective psychological mechanism. The hostage denies that this traumatic event is actually happening. They may view the event as a dream, thus having no basis in reality.

2. Delusions of Reprieve

The hostage slowly accepts the facts at hand and then begins to view the situation as temporary. The hostage believes that their freedom will arrive soon.

3. Busy Work

If freedom does not come quickly, the hostage usually begins some form of busy work. He will usually busy himself with an activity, which he feels comfortable doing, e.g.; counting ceiling tiles or mentally reciting memorized book passages, etc.

4. Taking Stock of Their Life

The final stage occurs when the hostage begins to take stock of their life. The hostage vows to do things differently in the future in an attempt to change for the better.

The Officer as a Hostage

An officer taken hostage should avoid turning into a "super cop." Do not forget the fact that you pose a threat in the hostage taker's mind simply because you are an officer. This point should not be heightened; therefore, be human in you demeanor. Project the image of a person who can accept adversity with dignity. Do not display bravado; this may provoke cruelty from the hostage taker. Nor should you show cowardice; this may provoke contempt. Understand that the hostage taker will issue orders and directions to you and that you will have to comply with them willingly or by force.

Behavior as a Hostage

While held hostage, there will most probably be times when you and the hostage taker speak to each other. Generally speak only if spoken to and never provoke your captor. Do not become argumentative or give the hostage taker any reason to grow angry. Attempt to answer any questions truthfully. Above all, do not attempt to negotiate with the hostage taker. You may inadvertently interfere with trained negotiators from the outside who will be endeavoring to gain rapport and trust with the hostage taker.

Depending upon the total length of the incident, personal goal setting is an essential survival technique. A hostage must place in their own mind certain obtainable items that they wish to accomplish. Certain tasks, such as eating, exercising (if possible) and shaving (if allowed), are vital in maintaining a healthy outlook and preparedness for a rescue attempt. Although the major goal of a hostage is survival, these minor obtainable goals are also vital.

As a hostage, you must never doubt that you will be rescued. Understand that the police, along with trained negotiators, have perfected their talents to a point where these types of incidents have been brought to successful outcomes, time and time again. Truly believe that, given time, the incident will be terminated and you will be safely released. The first two hours of any hostage incident are the most dangerous. Tension, stress and anxiety are all extremely high in the hostage taker, hostages and rescue personnel. As time progresses, the hostage and his captor have the opportunity to emotionally bond, and in general, calm down. As long as you understand that the longer the incident lasts, the better prepared a rescue attempt will be, your general outlook will be better and more oriented toward survival.

In other words, attempt to display a non-troublesome and rational attitude as a hostage. This is accomplished by keeping a basically high morale. In doing so you are projecting an atmosphere of order and calm in the center of a bizarre event.

While negotiations are actively taking place, assault plans are being drawn and reviewed. During the incident make an effort to locate yourself away from windows and doors. Naturally, if a rescue attempt is initiated, these two avenues are the most commonly used entrances. Further, if there are additional hostages; try to remain as close together as possible. This facilitates better communication between the hostages and better control by the rescuers if an assault is made.

The hostage taker is tense and extremely nervous. Abrupt movements made by the hostages tend to cause startled reactions by their captor(s), which may cause negative results. During the hostage incident, continue to mentally record all events that transpire. Note the hostage taker's general demeanor, weapons, appearance, name, etc. Determine which individuals seem to be in charge. If a crime occurs in your presence (assault, battery, etc.), note all the specifics surrounding the incident. Think twice about attempting to intercede; this may cause you additional problems, while not actually assisting the victim.

Every hostage incident is different. There may be times where you have the opportunity to overpower and gain control of the hostage taker. If this opportunity presents itself, remember you will have only one chance to carry it out. If unsuccessful, prepare for and expect swift retaliation. Likewise, you will have only one chance to execute an escape. Failing will result in some type of retribution. No one can state when or where to execute a plan to overpower the hostage taker or to try to escape. But, one statement should be made: If you truly feel that you have a chance to do either, a total 110% effort must be made. Anything less may result in failure.

If the termination of the incident results in a rescue attempt, be prepared to respond both physically and mentally to the rescuers.

Ending the Incident

Hostage incidents may be terminated in one of two ways. A negotiated settlement is the preferred conclusion; this occurs when rapport and trust are built between the hostage taker and the rescuers (negotiators).

When this occurs, do not be surprised to be secured and transported out of the area before or after the hostage taker is placed into custody. Remember that the rescue team may not know you and therefore, may treat you as a possible suspect or accomplice until your identity is made clear. The main concept is to follow all directions given to you by the rescue team. The less preferred method to terminate a hostage incident is tactical. This occurs when there is a breakdown in negotiations and the Incident Commander orders an assault. Immediately upon the rescuer's entrance, you should fall to the floor and be motionless. Ideally, cover should be sought. It is extremely important for you to comply with any and all directions issued by the rescue team. Once again, expect to be secured and moved out of the area until you are identified.

Debriefing

In all instances, released hostages must be interviewed and debriefed. Valuable information may be obtained through intelligence supplied by these former hostages. Law Enforcement Officer/Correctional Officers serve as excellent sources of reliable information in these types of situations. After a thorough debriefing, you should be examined by a physician or therapist in order to ascertain your physical and mental condition. This is imperative to assure your future welfare. There have been instances where officers have been held hostage, released and immediately sent back to work. This is not the ideal situation. As a freed hostage, be prepared to experience a tremendous release of emotions. You may laugh or cry; you may be extremely excited or completely drained. All these reactions are acceptable and should be looked upon as normal.

In this day and age, hostage incidents have become almost commonplace. Our Correctional Institutions mirror our society in what is good and what is bad. One must accept the concept that even if we provide good living conditions, good food, clean clothes, and excellent interpersonal communication skills, hostage incidents still arise. Hostile inmates may willingly throw all this away for a cause. You, as a Law Enforcement and Correctional Officer, may suffer because of that. You are viewed either as "tools" to be used for forcing inmates demands or "symbols" of an Institution or way of life that inmates despise. Whichever the case, your only response is to be trained, physically and mentally, to confront the issue and to survive.

CHAPTER 14 REVIEW QUESTIONS

1. Who are inmates afraid of?

   • Other inmates

   • Staff members

2. What are the two methods of terminating hostage incidents?

   • Negotiating

   • Tactical

3. True or False - Correctional Institutions in and of themselves may cause hostage situations to occur.

   • True

4. True or False - When inmates cannot adjust or cope with institutional life, rebellion takes place, which may culminate in a hostage situation.

   • True

5. True or False - If you are taken hostage, you should turn into a "supercop" because you are an officer and as such, are required to maintain control and discipline.

   • False

RELEASED HOSTAGES

POST-TRAUMA AND CARE

A number of years ago, it became apparent that those involved in shooting incidents were emotionally affected for some time after the incident itself. More and more research went into the care and treatment of those individuals in an attempt to assist them in regaining their emotional stability and helping them return to a productive professional career. As the years passed, those in the psychological field discovered that shooting incidents were not the only events which brought about trauma to the victims.

REACTIONS OF RELEASED HOSTAGES

Released hostages carry with them emotional scars that must be dealt with in order to ensure the mental stability of the victim. It is therefore extremely important to understand the various traumatic side effects caused by hostage taking incidents. The most dominant symptom of the victim is "Reactive Depression," which refers to the inability to express anger against their captors out of fear of re-experiencing the hostage role. Some of the traits associated with this include a passive nature at work and in their home environment, caused by a general "I Don't Care" type of attitude. Next, the released hostage experiences lackluster emotions and possible crying spells. Lastly, the individual may display a complete disinterest in a former gratification such as sexual contact, children, work and career expectations. In other words, a completely neutral attitude concerning pleasures they once truly enjoyed.

Night Terrors

A second symptom that released hostages encounter is "Night Terrors" or the universal fear of subjects breaking into their bedroom and recapturing them. Simply put, these are nothing more than vivid nightmares, which result in insomnia and chronic daytime tiredness.

Sexual Upset

"Sexual Upset" may also appear in released hostages causing a great deal of problems in their personal life. The loss of one's libido results in inadequate sexual attempts and sexual impotence. Additionally, individuals may be affected by the fear they experienced while being held captive and being open to homosexual attack.

Anxiety Apprehension

The last type of symptom which arises is labeled "Anxiety Apprehension", which is the basic fear of returning to work in the same location where the initial incident occurred. This initiates a feeling of fear in interacting with inmates, with who may be the same inmates, which were involved in the initial hostage incident.

The released hostage may feel depressed, emotionally upset and exhibit various modifications in their judgement and behavior.

TREATMENT OF RELEASED HOSTAGES

Knowing the problems that may be experienced by released hostages is just half the issue that must be acknowledged and dealt with in an effective manner. Certain responsibilities and actions should be implemented in order to assure the mental health of the individuals involved, beginning with their employer's administration.

Administrative Support

After an incident involving a hostage taking, the released victim is looking for a show of support, understanding and concern from their administrative staff. Administration should show support and admiration for the manner in which the released hostage conducted themselves during the incident, thereby validating the experience in the mind of the victim and returning to them their self-esteem and ego which had been drained by the incident.

All this can be effectively accomplished by issuing letters of commendation, making hospital visits to those who have been injured during the incident and holding individual meetings with the victims. An essential aspect of post-hostage treatment is the "Debriefing." This allows the victim to decompress and share their feelings, fears and anxieties with sympathetic individuals. Information, which is revealed by the released hostage, becomes invaluable to the prosecution of the hostage taker. Having this debriefing as soon as possible after the end of the event is more beneficial than waiting until a later date because the experience is fresher in the mind of the victim.

Returning to Work

Released hostages being debriefed immediately after the incident.

Eventually the released hostage will be returning to work therefore, considerations must be made regarding the individual's working environment.

Generally speaking, victims should return to work as soon as possible which, unfortunately in some instances, may be never. The trauma, deep-seated feelings and psychological impact of this type of event may affect individuals to such an extent that they may never regain the ability to return to a functional position in their former job.

If however, they do return, care must be given to where they are logistically placed. Should they return directly to the same area where they experienced the traumatic event? Should they be placed in the same position, dealing with the same individuals who may have been involved in the event? These are some of the questions, which must be answered in addition to options made available for their placement into the workplace. In short, some released hostages may return to their jobs and continue to be quite effective while others may be completely unable to ever return to their previous job.

Prosecution of Hostage Takers

In all cases the individuals guilty of holding the victims against their will should and must be prosecuted. These responsible subjects must be taken before the judicial process and prosecuted to the full extent of the law for a number of reasons. By taking this action, the released hostages are relieved of some of the anger and depression they experienced during and immediately after the incident. Additionally, by viewing the prosecution process, the victims come to the realization that their ordeal was not in vain. In short, the concept would be that society would be redeeming the victim's traumatic experience.

Post-Hostage Counseling

In the continuing concern for the mental health of the released hostages, further assistance should be offered in the form of a "Post-Hostage Counseling Team." This team is composed of a group of individuals who may have at some point in time been held hostage themselves.

This group of individuals would ideally be trained in interpersonal communications and counseling techniques so that they may be efficient in their meetings with the released hostages. It is also recommended that a trained psychologist be a working member of this group.

Collectively, the members of the team would meet with any and all released hostages so that the victims may be available to discuss the incident and the personal feelings they may have. In turn, this would facilitate the ventilating and alleviating of fear and anxiety being experienced by the released hostages. Obviously, if problems exist and continue for some time, professional help should be administered.

CHAPTER 15 REVIEW QUESTIONS

1. State the four types of traumatic side effects, which may be experienced by a released hostage.

   • Reactive Depression

   • Night Terrors

   • Sexual Upset

   • Anxiety Apprehension

2. Which side effect causes an inability to express anger against the captors?

   • Reactive Depression

3. Which side effect results in the fantasy of subjects breaking into your room and recapturing you?

   • Night Terrors

4. Which side effect causes loss of your libido?

   • Sexual Upset

5. Which side effect may cause you to have a fear of returning to work in the same location where the incident occurred?

   • Anxiety/Apprehension

6. True or False - Your employer must show support of the released hostage after the incident, thereby validating the experience in the mind of the victim.

   • True

7. True or False - A debriefing is not really a necessary aspect of post-hostage treatment.

   • False

8. True or False - Released hostages should be returned to work as soon as possible, based upon their ability to function in their environment.

   • True

9. True or False - A post-hostage counseling team is just one method of assisting the released hostage in returning to a productive position in the work force.

   • True

DEBRIEFINGS

As in any police action, debriefings are a vital part of a critical incident. In the realm of hostage/hostage-related incidents, there are actually two separate types of debriefings that may be reviewed. The first is the basic debriefing of released hostages, suspects and witnesses. In dealing with this type of situation, the ability to perform basic "interrogation" becomes a vital element in the big picture. We must understand that information may be obtained that will be factual thus, leading to a successful outcome of the situation or erroneous, which may cause miscalculations and in turn, a less than acceptable outcome of the situation. A case in point surrounds the 1971 Olympic Games in Munich, Germany. In this incident, information was received regarding the number of suspects involved. The information stated that there were five suspects when in reality, there were eight or more. This caused an insufficient amount of snipers to be deployed which without question, contributed to the ultimate death of all of the hostages.

Obviously, depending upon where the incident is taking place, more or less information may be readily available. If you find yourself facing an incident in a familiar location, such as inside a jail, convenience store, public building, etc., you may and probably will already have the basic layout of the incident location. However, even if this is the case, you still must determine the specific facts of the situation such as, how many hostages are present, who are they, are there any weapons present, etc.

If you are called upon to debrief individuals during hostage related situations; you must keep in mind the basic dynamics of the environment from which individuals have just emerged. In other words, the emotional state of the individual must be acknowledged. In many cases, released hostage's experience what we have discussed as the "Stockholm Syndrome," the psychological bonding between the suspect and the victim (hostage), causing the victim to protect the suspect and in general, sympathize with him. In a case like this, the information you received may be inaccurate or at least, tainted. Care must be taken when this type of intelligence is incorporated into forming a response, either tactically or by negotiations. Taking the above into consideration, individuals who are being debriefed should be kept separate from each other during the process. In this way, the released hostages do not taint each other's information with perceptions of their own. By interviewing individuals separately, intelligence can be confirmed by more than one source in order to check for accuracy and consistency.

DEBRIEFING QUESTIONS

With the above in mind, your first consideration is to determine what information should be obtained during the debriefing. Normally, the Command Staff will have a series of questions that they must have answered as quickly as possible. These will most often be basic factual points, which will assist them in maintaining control and accuracy regarding the implemented responses. Even though this may be the primary quest of Command, do not let their input delay negatively affect you process. In other words, you should maximize the time spent debriefing an individual.

An effective procedure to utilize is to create a formalized questionnaire containing general questions, which may be common to all hostage-related situations. This in turn will keep you on track during the process. Prior to the debriefing, you may review the questionnaire and not the information, which you feel, should be obtained as soon as possible. For example, how many suspects are involved, how many victims, any weapons what type of weapons, any injuries, etc. After all this primary information is obtained, secondary issues may be addressed which may be utilized at a later time.

The main issue is to keep in mind is to debrief individuals as quickly as possible after they have been removed from the crisis scene. By doing this, the events that had taken place are fresh in the subject's mind. Also, this eliminates the problem of individuals attempting to remember events after some time has passed, causing the possibility of inaccurate information. This presents important information immediately for use by the negotiators and tactical personnel alike.

DEBRIEFING CHECK-LIST

Interviewer: _____

Date / Time _____ / _____

I. Interviewee Information

A. Name: _____

B. Address: _____

C. Phone #: _____

D. Social Security #: _____

E. Date of Birth: _____

II. Injuries

A. Type:_____

B. First Aid:

  1. Type: _____

  2. Supplied by: _____

C. Transported:

  1. To: _____

  2. By: _____

III. Suspect(s): (number?)

A. Name / Moniker: _____

B. Description:

1. Height / Weight: _____ / _____

2. Hair / Eyes:_____ / _____

3. Approx. Age: _____

4. Tatoos: _____

C. Location: _____

   1. Ingress / Egress: _____

D. Observation Points:

   1. Of us by suspect: _____

E. Weapons:

   1. Type(s):

     a. Handgun: _____

     b. Long Gun: _____

     c. Knife: _____

     d. Explosive: _____

     e. Other: _____

   2. Number / Caliber / Type: _____

F. Violence Potential:

   1. Threatened: _____

   2. Completed: _____

G. Injured:

   1. Yes / How: _____

   2. No: _____

IV. Other Victims: (Hostages)

A. Number: _____

B. Name(s): _____

C. Description(s): _____

D. Physical Condition: _____

E. Mental Attitude(s): _____

V. Drawing Of Suspect / Hostage Location:

VI. Additional Information:

DEBRIEFING DYNAMICS

Considering all the factors involved in a debriefing, the most important is the individual who is actually asking the questions, the Debriefer. You may wish to utilize skilled interrogators in this position, especially if they can adapt their style to meet the demand. They must understand that emotions play a significant role in this type of situation. Many times, released hostages have been physically and mentally abused during they're captivity thus, suffering damaging psychological effects.

Debriefers must also be able to suppress any type of reactions, including facial reactions, to any atrocities subjects may describe. Skilled interrogators are quite natural in a question and answer environment therefore, this type of debriefing should not be all that unfamiliar to them. Even with this in mind, you may wish to have a member of the negotiating team performs the actual debriefing, based upon their training and interpersonal communication skills.

EVALUATING INFORMATION

For obvious reasons, it is essential for you to ascertain whether the individual being debriefed is relating accurate information to you. You must be certain that this information is actually available to the individual as first-hand knowledge or whether they "believe" the fact to be true. For example, was there enough light in the room for the individual to actually see the item in question? Was there enough light for the individual to accurately describe in detail the item in question? Did the individual relate what they "saw" or "heard?" Are the other senses (smell, hearing) being used to compensate for what the individual believes happened? Answers to these questions will determine the true accuracy of the information gathered.

One method to help confirm whether debriefed individuals are indeed relating accurate information is to ask "control questions." These are questions for which you already know the answers. In other words, factual intelligence gathered through detailed building plans, tactical recognizance, etc. will offer solid information. By asking debriefed individuals questions pertaining to these issues, you may determine if they are lying, exaggerating, or simply an unreliable witness. Keep in mind that individuals involved in a critical incident, may be telling you what they "think" happened their "perception" of the event. Because of this distortions may occur. However, if you discover the debriefed individual is actually lying, you may wish to search for a motive for the deception and compare the stories of other released hostages.

Debriefing an individual involved in a hostage-related incident requires the same degree of planning, as does any tactical maneuver. Therefore, every attempt should be made to obtain adequate, accurate and necessary information.

The previous paragraphs dealt with the debriefings of individuals during a hostage/hostage-related situation. The second type of debriefing occurs after the entire incident is over. Those officers who become involved in these critical incidents should attend a "Group

Psychological Debriefing," a "Group Tactical Debriefing" and an "Incident Clarification Debriefing."

GROUP PSYCHOLOGICAL DEBRIEFING

This should be voluntary in nature, where those attending feel no obligation to speak if they do not wish to participate. This debriefing should include all those personnel who were present and possibly, their spouses. Issues covered during the gathering surround the emotional effects of the event and how they may relate to you and your spouse and family. For obvious reasons, this debriefing should be conducted after all legal issues surrounding the event are over.

GROUP TACTICAL DEBRIEFING

This is the operational critique of the event; the "down and dirty" review of what happened. This gathering provides the chain of command with feedback and reasons why specific actions were taken. It assists in identifying proficiencies and weaknesses of personnel, leaders and units in addition to, determining what should be done differently during future events. During this debriefing, avoid detailed examinations of issues not directly related to the event, discussing instead what took place and why. Do not overemphasize mistakes. Stress strong points and good performance thus, making the gathering a positive experience.

INCIDENT CLARIFICATION DEBRIEFING

As we have discussed in chapter 5, during any type of critical incident, inaccurate and sometimes misleading information tends to reach the media and in turn the citizens of the community. This debriefing should be conducted after all of the issues are reviewed and investigated at which time, media representatives are contacted and advised of the actual facts of the event, in as much detail as is possible.

CHAPTER 16 REVIEW QUESTIONS

1. Who is the most important individual involved in a debriefing?

   • The individual directing the debriefing; the facilitator

2. When should debriefings be conducted?

   • As soon as possible after the termination of the incident, when all issues are reviewed and investigated

3. True or False - Individuals should be debriefed as quickly as possible after they have been removed from the crisis scene.

   • True

4. True or False - For obvious reasons it is essential for you to ascertain whether the individual being debriefed is relating accurate information.

   • True

5. True or False - Debriefing an individual does not require obtaining adequate, accurate or necessary information.

   • False

CONCLUSION

Even after reviewing, understanding and employing all of the basic concepts put forth in this text, when confronted with hostage/hostage-related incidents, we can offer no absolute guarantee of success. In situations like these, numerous factors enter into a successful outcome. The particular individuals who are involved, the specific location of the incident, the available equipment, the number of trained personnel who are deployed, the effectiveness of pre-planning and scenario training, and the determination and commitment of all involved personnel all contribute to the end result. These, along with additional factors, will ultimately dictate the final outcome.

In short, this text serves as a sound, basic beginning to a successful conclusion of a crisis incident. In the final assessment however, it will fall upon those who are performing their respective duties to determine whether they have succeeded in doing their best. To those individuals, we offer our admiration and support.

NOTES

NOTES

NOTES

NOTES

HOSTAGE SEMINARS

WHO SHOULD ATTEND?

Law enforcement and correctional officers who are negotiators, supervisors, academy training instructors, line officers, correctional housing officer, response team personnel, and all other personnel involved in planning for and responding to hostage situations.

TOPICS COVERED

Crisis Intervention: First Officer	Negotiation vs. Tactical Response
Command Post Guidelines	Reason for Hostage Situations
Incident Command System	Hostage Survival
Mob Psychology and Control	Post Trauma
Response Teams	

This course is designed to assist the participants in learning how to defuse hostile situations using proven crisis intervention and negotiation techniques. They will become aware of the dynamics of hostage situations, and how to relate to them as a first responder. Command Post and Incident Command Systems will be discussed. We will explore the Response Team's responsibilities in regards to the issue of Negotiation vs. Tactical. Participants will understand why hostage situations occur, the risk of being taken hostage, and the odds for survival. Participants will learn viable hostage survival techniques and physical and mental strategies to cope with the problem of being a hostage. Post Trauma will focus on the after care for the officer.

We have assisted many jurisdictions over the years by providing comprehensive in-house training programs for their staff. We can provide the above listed training, *HOSTAGE: How To Negotiate, Manage, and Survive*, for your personnel ON-SITE. If you have personnel that require training in this subject and you cannot send them on the road for that training, we'll come to you.

For additional information, please call Cecil Pearson & Associates, Inc. at **(702) 645-3166 Tel/Fax**, or e-mail **peaccc@aol.com**